Even great leaders with outstanding records of achievement can struggle in new and difficult circumstances. *GUTS* provides a deep understanding of how our minds process stress and the actions and behaviors required to optimize performance. It's a must-read for developing leaders and high performing teams in these challenging times.

—CLAUDIA SAN PEDRO, President of SONIC Drive-In

I have studied and coached top performers in the Navy SEALs and in Fortune 500 companies. In *GUTS*, Ed Hiner shows you what it takes to be successful. Evidence-based and practical, this book is for anyone who aspires to be better.

—JOSH COTTON, PhD, former Personnel Research
Psychologist to the Navy SEALs and coauthor
of *The Talent War*

GUTS presents vivid insight into the education, training, and experiences of a Navy SEAL from a Navy SEAL—with correlations that are applicable to all of us in both business and everyday life. Ed's ability to illustrate disciplined personal growth and genuine accountability with a team-oriented focus is the foundation of leadership.

—JERRY DIPOTO, General Manager of the Seattle Mariners

GUTS is not just inspirational; it's a life-transforming program that shows you how to manufacture motivation and create discipline. If you *do* what Iron Ed says, you will be on your way to excellence, whether in the Major Leagues or in your career. Like the Moneyball season changed baseball forever, this book will change how people understand mental toughness and deal with fear under tremendous stress. These life-transforming strategies should be taught to everyone early, but it's never too late to learn!

—RICK PETERSON, Pitching Coach of the
"Moneyball" Oakland A's

Lieutenant Commander Brian Hiner has written the best motivational book I have read in the past 30 years. In *GUTS*, he presents hard-earned, life-changing wisdom that all can apply to build their future.

—WAYNE WEINER, DEd, Senior Consultant at
the National Institutes of Health

In *GUTS*, warrior leader Ed Hiner shares his heart and soul. It is an invaluable guide on how to overcome, how to compete, and how to win when the odds are stacked up against you. I will be passing it along to several hundred of my corporate teammates.

—MITCH LITTLE, SVP of Worldwide Client Engagement
at Microchip Technology Inc.

Hiner has taken the extraordinary life he's led, broken it down into simple understandable concepts, and given us a guide to overcome fear in all aspects of our lives, so we can actually achieve success. Everyone should read *GUTS*!

—JIM CLEMENTE, retired FBI Supervisory Special Agent
and profiler and writer and producer of *Criminal Minds*

For five years, I served with the Navy SEALs as an Iraqi warrior during the height of the Iraq War. SEALs are my brothers, and they proved that they are the best of the best during the most dangerous missions. Iron Ed captures the essence of the mind of the Navy SEAL, and if you want to learn mental toughness and seek excellence in life, *GUTS* is the book for you. His no-nonsense Blue-Collar Scholar approach describes the mental toughness and character that I saw during those five years in combat with my beloved brothers. HOOYAH, *GUTS*!

—RIYADH AHMED KHALAF AL AHMADY, *New York Times* bestselling author of *Code Name: Johnny Walker*

Captivating, with highly applicable concepts you can quickly implement, *GUTS* is a much-needed wake-up call for anyone asleep at the wheel in life. Ed lights a fire under you to get up and take action on your most important goals.

—STACI REIDINGER, APR+M, US Marine Corps
Captain (ret.) and Cofounder of the San Diego
Business & Nonprofit Crisis Support Network

The timeless leadership wisdom in *GUTS*, so compellingly and vividly shared by Ed Hiner, offers an accelerated path toward living a true and authentic life of plenty, in which our conscious actions and free choices lead to our most desired outcomes.

—JOHAN SCHOTTE, Chairman of the
Johan Schotte Foundation

Lieutenant Commander Ed Hiner has written a must-read book for anyone wanting to learn how to manage fear and motivate themselves to achieve at a higher level. In *GUTS*, you will learn principles for overall performance, success, and happiness.

—CRISTINA VERSARI, PhD, Founder and CEO of the
San Diego University for Integrative Studies and Director
of the Sport Psychology Program

Powerful! Iron Ed's Blue-Collar Scholar approach resonated with me because I believe all humans can better themselves through an insatiable curiosity for philosophy, science, art, psychology, and entrepreneurship. And, as the book makes clear, thinking is not enough; one must also be a practical doer.

—JEREMEY DONOVAN, SVP of Sales Strategy at SalesLoft
and bestselling author of *How to Deliver a TED Talk*

Everyone experiences stress, but nothing can be more stressful than when you are fighting for your life. Iron Ed teaches us how to handle, manage, and successfully overcome stress.

—EDDIE TANTOCO, CPA, former VP of
Starwood and Marriott Hotels, global business
consultant, and philanthropist

Iron Ed is a renowned operator and one of the most experienced trainers in SEAL history from one of the most elite organizations in the world. His understanding of the pursuit of excellence is what makes *GUTS* such a powerful training camp for the mind. From his Blue-Collar Scholar point of view, he not only tells you the importance of accountability, discipline, and motivation but also teaches you how to manufacture them. His final chapter, "AWE: Awaken the Warrior Energy" resonated deeply with me as it applied to the transition after my Olympic career. An exciting read, every page has unexpected nuggets of wisdom. It's simple: read this book, do what he says, and you'll improve in whatever you wish to achieve!

—RYAN BAILEY, three-time men's water polo College
All-American, four-time Olympian, Olympic silver
medalist, and USA Water Polo Hall of Famer

As an Olympian and professional volleyball player, turned medical device executive, turned expat digital marketing entrepreneur, I've reinvented myself several times throughout the years. Ed Hiner's *GUTS* resonated deeply with me. More than just a great read, it lays out powerful principles—taking complete ownership of your predicament and outcome, embracing the Blue-Collar Scholar mentality, and creating habits of attitude—that will open up the world of possibility to you.

—MIKE LAMBERT, 2-time Olympian (men's indoor
volleyball), 16-time AVP champion, 2004 MVP of
the AVP, and Beach Volleyball Hall of Famer

U.S. Navy SEALs are among the most successful elite organizations in the world. Iron Ed's unique approach captures how to master life and achieve greatness under tremendous stress, no matter what your profession. In the BMX world, we also learned to use fear as a tool, rather than a hindrance, in order to succeed and complete the task at hand. Ed brings this home to all of us with battlefield lessons. Do what Lieutenant Commander Hiner says, and you'll be on your way to excellence.

—TJ Lavin, host of MTV's *The Challenge* and
professional BMX rider

Most books teach leadership theory, and while it's good to know and understand what leadership is and isn't, what's more important is knowing how to apply it. In this book, Ed teaches you just that. *GUTS* a practical, pragmatic, and proven hands-on guide to achieving results when under pressure. This should be compulsory reading for anyone thinking about taking up a leadership position.

—Gordon Tredgold, author of *FAST: 4 Principles
Every Business Needs to Achieve Success and Drive Results*

Ed Hiner was handed a tough mission. The retired Navy SEAL— and natural-born storyteller—has breathed rarefied air, receiving elite training and living through experiences to which few people can relate. In writing *GUTS*, Hiner wanted to share his expertise about turning difficulty into success with all of us, and that meant telling stories that are not just informative and enjoyable but also relatable. He pulled it off. The concept is solid and creative. The writing is clean and clear, and Hiner avoids the quicksand into which other writers tend to fall. Mission accomplished, Frogman. Well done.

—Ruben Navarrette, Syndicated Columnist of the
Washington Post Writers Group and author of *A Darker
Shade of Crimson: Odyssey of a Harvard Chicano*

There are three kinds of people in the world. There are those who make things happen, those who watch things happen, and those who look around after the fact and say, "What happened?" Clearly, only one of those categories leads to success and happiness. Leaving one's life to dumb luck ("What happened?"), or worse, living as though we have no control over our lives and circumstances (watching what happens) is not the path.

Ed's book is a field manual for making things happen in our lives. Few people have more credentials to understand what it means and what it takes. His experience as a SEAL and his personal background have put him in a position to share insights from which we can all benefit. The concepts he shares are universal. They apply to all of us, regardless of the challenges we face. Each chapter details an essential component to the toolkit we all need to be great.

Over my three decades as an educator (teacher, site administrator, district leader), I have worked with kids from all walks of life whose potential has been compromised by their life circumstances or, more significantly, their approach to their life circumstances. In most cases, it's not their fault—they didn't have the toolkit. As educators, our real job is to prepare our students to be successful in whatever endeavors they choose, to become experts at becoming experts. Our tendency is to focus on subject matter content, even though we have no idea what they will do in their futures. We can certainly do more to help all kids maximize their potential, and the information in Ed's book is precisely what they need to know to assure success in whatever endeavors they choose. I highly recommend adding Ed's book to every teacher's library and incorporating his teachings into our classrooms.

—MIKE VOLLMERT, EdD

Iron Ed Hiner identifies how dangerous living in fear can be, but more importantly, he tells us how to transform fear into motivation. A truly timely read!

—GRAHAM LEDGER, host of *The Ledger Report*

GUTS

GREATNESS UNDER
TREMENDOUS STRESS

A Navy SEAL's System for Turning Fear
into Accomplishment

BRIAN "IRON ED" HINER

Mc
Graw
Hill

NEW YORK   CHICAGO   SAN FRANCISCO   ATHENS   LONDON
MADRID   MEXICO CITY   MILAN   NEW DELHI
SINGAPORE   SYDNEY   TORONTO

1 2 3 4 5 6 7 8 9   LCR   26 25 24 23 22 21

ISBN 978-1-260-46292-0
MHID   1-260-46292-7

e-ISBN 978-1-260-46293-7
e-MHID   1-260-46293-5

Design by Lee Fukui and Mauna Eichner

Library of Congress Cataloging-in-Publication Data

Names: Hiner, Ed, author.
Title: GUTS: greatness under tremendous stress : a Navy SEAL's system for
  turning fear into accomplishment / Brian «Iron Ed» Hiner.
Description: New York : McGraw Hill, [2021] | Includes bibliographical
  references and index.
Identifiers: LCCN 2020043611 (print) | LCCN 2020043612 (ebook) | ISBN
  9781260462920 (hardback) | ISBN 9781260462937 (ebook)
Subjects: LCSH: Hiner, Ed. | United States. Navy. SEALs—Biography. |
  Achievement motivation. | Resilience (Personality trait) |
  Success—Psychological aspects. | Fear.
Classification: LCC BF503 .H55 2021 (print) | LCC BF503 (ebook) | DDC
  158.1—dc23
LC record available at https://lccn.loc.gov/2020043611
LC ebook record available at https://lccn.loc.gov/2020043612

McGraw Hill books are available at special quantity discounts to use as premiums and sales promotions or for use in corporate training programs. To contact a representative, please visit the Contact Us pages at www.mhprofessional.com.

To my son, Jake, and my wife, Wendy.
And to the children of the world and to veterans—
I have seen the horrors of war borne by the most innocent
and those who risk their lives for each other.

CONTENTS

PREFACE

"Now what?" I asked myself right after my first book, *First, Fast, Fearless*, became a *Los Angeles Times* bestseller. Believe it or not, that was the lowest point of my life. I had grown up poor, and by the age of 12, I lived full time with my grandmother and my brother deep in the Blue Ridge Mountains of Virginia. My grandmother only had a seventh-grade education, but she was tough and she had guts. Growing up in poverty and coming from a broken home is a lonely experience, and it permeates all aspects of life with fear, doubt, and a sense of scarcity.

Baseball saved me. My coach, Coach Cutler, took a chance on me, and I made varsity as a freshman in high school. Baseball gave me direction in life; it gave me the first glimpse of a future. I was awarded a Division One baseball college scholarship and was inducted into the Virginia High School Hall of Fame.

The thought of graduating from college was overwhelming. I was in uncharted territory, and I was on my own. But as luck would have it, I ran into a Navy SEAL. He told me about a life of adventure, mystery, and danger; about the ultimate team that was also a family. A light went on in me. This was what I was searching for. This was my calling. I hitchhiked from Virginia Beach to Richmond. A day later, I signed up!

Twenty years, three wars, and nine tours later, in 2012, I retired from the SEAL Teams. I was happy—at least I thought I was. A few months after retiring, my dad died suddenly. Although I had a hard childhood, coming from a broken family, my dad and I had since repaired our relationship. No matter the circumstances, he had a special place in my heart. Most boys look up to their fathers as if they are Superman. I was no different. Although my dad had his flaws, I felt like he was my protector, my anchor. Just knowing he was there gave me a sense of safety. And then he was gone.

Less than six months later, I lost my brother—the one person I had grown up with who had known me all of my life. He, too, was gone. In a short period, I had lost my identity as a SEAL, my team, and my family. My friends and teammates were getting killed or wounded or, worse, killing themselves. I was diagnosed with post-traumatic stress disorder (PTSD), traumatic brain injury (TBI), and numerous physical injuries. I had lost my "why."

There's an Ernest Hemingway quote I found myself living: "There is no hunting like the hunting of man and those who have hunted armed men long enough and liked it, never really care for anything else thereafter." Having a dangerous profession and serving in combat—that is very unique. When you are done with it, life is very different. It's like deep scuba diving for long periods: the diver doesn't get the bends while he is down; he gets the bends when he comes to the surface. The longer you stay down, the worse it is when you surface.

After retiring I felt like I had bolted to the surface with no real transition, and then it all compounded. Being a SEAL and going into combat is addicting, and like most addictions, it's a love-hate relationship. The taste for it is there, probably for life, even though I know it's bad for me. It numbed me to happiness and joy. It took away my feelings and my connectedness to the best parts of my life and to the people who meant the most to me.

There were times I couldn't sleep for 72 hours without medication, and many of the medications didn't work. I was always nervous and in a fearful state of mind. I was full of anger and hatred for my enemies. It was controlling my life and stealing my joy. I felt like I was in a downward spiral. One of the final straws was when I started to hear whispering at night while I was in bed. I would get up and clear the house to ensure there were no intruders. At times I thought I could see movements in the shadows. I knew it was irrational, but I felt like "they" were coming to get me.

Everything around me was crumbling. I had lost my identity, my team, my meaningful mission, and my overall well-being. I had lost so many of my SEAL brothers and two of my closest family members. My world was in tatters. What held it together was my single-minded focus on writing my first book, *First, Fast, Fearless*. I had always been motivated by a meaningful mission, so after I had accomplished my goal, after the book was published and became a bestseller, it all came crashing down. I was wracked by fear and self-doubt about the future, about what would come next.

Warriors don't feel sorry for themselves; they are not victims, yet I started down that path. I knew I had to pick myself up by my bootstraps. I knew I had to start living again. I had to fulfill the promises I had made to myself in war—and now I am. And I did that using the principles in *GUTS*, which I now want to share with you. Everything I write about in this book is drawn from my own journey. I hope it will teach you how to turn fear into accomplishment so that you can achieve whatever goals you've set for yourself—and lead happier, more successful, more fulfilled lives.

HOOYAH! Let's do this!

ACKNOWLEDGMENTS

Countless people—too many to identify by name—over the years have helped me get to where I am, and I will forever be grateful to each and every one of them. In the interest of brevity, I would like to highlight a select few.

To my family—my son, Jake, my wife, Wendy, and my dog and therapist, Rosebud—for once again listening to all my stories and ideas ad nauseam.

To Matt Heckemeyer and Rhett Fisher, for always being there to help motivate me to write and being my best friends and brothers.

To all my SEAL brothers and my brothers and sisters in the armed services, I love you and thank you for all you do.

To my partners and friends who helped me develop the SEALpreneurship program, using GUTS principles, that serve underserved children—Charles Parisi, David Varcardipone, Gary Denham, and Mike Vollmert—thank you for serving.

To the San Diego courts and juvenile school system, thank you for allowing me to fulfill a promise to myself, helping the kids at San Pasqual Academy for foster youth.

To all the kids at San Pasqual Academy, thank you for allowing us to serve you and inspiring us to be better people.

To my extended family—the Driscolls, Hiners, and Borkums—thank you for being in my corner.

To my colleague Peter Sander, once again, thank you for helping bring this project to life.

I'm fortunate to have a great publisher, McGraw Hill, with an excellent staff and the best editor in the business, Casey Ebro. Thank you.

Lastly, I would like to thank all the readers and leaders who are willing to pick up this book with an openness to learning how to become a better leader and, hopefully, a better you.

INTRODUCTION

The Origin of GUTS (Greatness Under Tremendous Stress)

When I started my own "journey home" after 20 years of service, I reflected on my days as a lead instructor, training people to become U.S. Navy SEALs, a time I will always remember with reverence and awe. Navy SEAL training is known to be one of the toughest and most rigorous military training regimens in the world. At the height of the wars on terror, we received nearly 10,000 applications a year; of those, we could accept only 1,200 or so to even begin training. Attrition is high, and the most we have ever graduated in a year is 250 SEALs. The odds of getting in and making it through to graduation are low.

Our Basic Underwater Demolition/SEAL (BUD/S) training is what most people think of when they think of SEAL training, but BUD/S is just a portion of the complete basic training a student goes through to become a Navy SEAL. Before students get their coveted Navy SEAL Trident, they must successfully complete more than a year of grueling training that includes:

- 8-week Naval Special Warfare Prep School

- 3-week Orientation

- 21-week Basic Underwater Demolition/SEAL (BUD/S) training (including Hell Week)

- 7-week Parachute Jump School and Survival, Evasion, Resistance, Escape (SERE)

- 19-week SEAL Qualification Training (SQT)

Upon graduation from SQT, a trainee receives the coveted Navy SEAL Trident, which officially designates him as a Navy SEAL. He receives a Special Warfare Operator Naval Rating or, in the case of a commissioned Naval officer, the designation Naval Special Warfare (SEAL) Officer. He is then assigned to a SEAL Team or a SEAL Delivery Vehicle (SDV) Team, and begins an 18-month predeployment training program consisting of:

- 6-month Professional Development (ProDev)— individual Specialty Training

- 6-month Unit Level Training (ULT)

- 6-month Squadron Integration Training

In total, this represents two-and-a-half to three years of continuous training until the new SEAL deploys for the first time—and then his journey truly begins.

An old wooden plaque inside the training compound reads: "The only easy day was yesterday." This expression sets clear expectations that being a SEAL is never easy; only yesterday is because it's over. After a six-month deployment, the 18-month predeployment training program starts over, and each time the SEAL conducts ProDev, he masters a new skill, such as explosive breaching; becoming a sniper, professional driver, or interrogator; leadership training; and more. As the SEAL continues to deploy, he develops new skills, but also retrains in the fundamental skills. His training and development are never complete.

When I look back to training SEALs, my mind always takes me to graduation, the day when students become Navy SEALs and join the brotherhood that we all genuinely love. For the first time, we see the students with their families and loved ones. In a sense, it's a clash of past and present, as students become aware of their own transformation, one that is also recognized by their families.

"My son is different now" was a common refrain, especially from the mothers, on graduation day. Something had changed, and it was noticeable. It was a moment to celebrate, but it was also a moment of sadness, of missing the son who used to be. It wasn't a physical transformation, but something else. The mothers would tell me that their son's presence had changed, that he now walked, talked, and carried himself differently, and that he addressed the world around him differently. It wasn't arrogance or cockiness: he had developed a different relationship with life and his place in it. From my perspective, he had developed GUTS—Greatness Under Tremendous Stress—a systematic approach to accomplishment that enables him to become an "alpha" in his professional and personal world.

This book is not about helping you become a SEAL (although if that's your intent, it certainly won't hurt). It's about helping you develop GUTS, so you can take an alpha approach to everything you do in life.

WHAT DO I MEAN BY "ALPHA"?

In the animal world, many species travel in packs led by an alpha male or female. The other animals in the pack always sense and know who the alpha is, just as the families can see and sense the change in their loved ones at graduation. From this interaction he can see and feel this transformation himself, and he has what I call the "alpha swagger"—a focused and authentic state of mind and a sense of being fully present, living life on his own terms with intent. This "swagger" isn't necessarily permanent—I felt I had lost some of it when I came home from my 20-year career.

GUTS AND THE
ACCOMPLISHMENT GAP

When I started to develop the GUTS concept, I dissected my life, studied what had worked in the past, and identified what had made me successful, happy, fulfilled, and thrive in such a dangerous and challenging profession. All of us have to deal with fear and stress and must manufacture the motivation to get ourselves past it. GUTS serves as a bridge to help you cross the accomplishment gaps in your life.

An accomplishment gap is simply a gap between who or what you are and who or what you think you should be or want to be. A "State of the American Workplace" Gallup poll shows that 70 percent of employees are either passively or actively disengaged with their work. Apathy is prevalent; people aren't motivated and thus waste their lives. These gaps pop up in our personal lives, too.

Now I don't recommend that everyone become a SEAL—it surely is not for everyone! What I do recommend is that you borrow the GUTS page from the SEAL playbook, and use GUTS and the alpha approach to deal with the accomplishment gaps in your professional and personal lives. Deal with fear, become a warrior, get it done, and learn from your success!

"A MESSAGE TO GARCIA"

Published in 1899 by Elbert Hubbard, the essay "A Message to Garcia" continues to be taught to this day at the United States Naval Academy in Annapolis, West Point, and virtually all Officer Training Programs in all branches of service. It tells a story that took place during the Spanish-American War of 1898, when the United States declared war against Spain due to Spanish interference in Cuba. The war was triggered by the sinking of the American battleship the USS *Maine*. After the sinking of the *Maine*, President William McKinley needed to make contact with the senior Cuban insurgency leader, General Calixto Garcia. As Hubbard wrote:

> In all this Cuban business there is one man stands out on the horizon of my memory like Mars at perihelion.
>
> When war broke out between Spain and the United States, it was very necessary to communicate quickly with the leader of the Insurgents. Garcia was somewhere in the mountain fastnesses [secluded places] of Cuba—no one knew where. No mail or telegraph could reach him. The President must secure his co-operation, and quickly.
>
> What to do!
>
> Someone said to the President, "There's a fellow by the name of Rowan will find Garcia for you, if anybody can."
>
> Rowan was sent for and given a letter to be delivered to Garcia. How "the fellow by name of Rowan" took the letter, sealed it up in an oil-skin pouch, strapped it over his heart, in four days landed by night off the coast of Cuba from an open boat, disappeared into the jungle, and in three weeks came out on the other side of the island, having traversed a hostile country on foot, and having delivered his letter to Garcia, are things I have no special desire now to tell in detail. The point I wish to make is this: McKinley gave

Rowan a letter to be delivered to Garcia; Rowan took the letter and did not ask, "Where is he at?"

By the Eternal! There is a man whose form should be cast in deathless bronze and the statue placed in every college in the land. It is not book-learning young men need, nor instruction about this or that, but a stiffening of the vertebrae which will cause them to be loyal to a trust, to act promptly, concentrate their energies; do the thing—"carry a message to Garcia!"[1]

First Lt. Andrew S. Rowan, a junior Army Officer, was entrusted this mission by his Commanding Officer directly from the president. He was given no guidance, no instructions; he was on his own. Rowan knew it and accepted it. He left by ship at night and landed soon after in Jamaica, where he met up with the head of the Cuban junta. A carriage drove up to him, and someone in Spanish said: "It is time!" Rowan was smuggled in a wagon across Jamaica and then transferred onto a small boat loaded with weapons to the island of Cuba. He cut through jungles and escaped and evaded the Spanish. He rode horses for days and was smuggled by unknown men he had never met and had no way of vetting. He encountered countless trials and tribulations, but he never stopped pressing forward. In the worst of times, he was at his best and delivered the message to Garcia.

He then carried a message back to the United States to help coordinate the war plans, and his actions proved critical to the war's success. One hundred years ago, Rowan was a household name. A Senate bill was drafted that called for a statue to commemorate his bravery and perseverance, and he received the Army's second-highest award, the Distinguished Service Cross.

Rowan's effort is timeless; that's why it's still taught today. His capacity for independent action, initiative, courage, and problem solving and his ability to perform during times of uncertainty and duress are legendary and something to aspire to. Rowan had GUTS!

BLUE-COLLAR SCHOLAR:
THE SCIENCE OF DOING

SEALs know that we will face difficulty, that we will be challenged in ways that we cannot predict, but that we must be prepared mentally and physically to carry the message. Before we can lead others, we must learn to lead ourselves. Beyond the distinct traits of physical and moral courage, a SEAL must learn how to become an expert at being an expert quickly. SEALs learn to be what I call "Blue-Collar Scholars."

The perfect Blue-Collar Scholar is a highly adaptable handyman with expertise in philosophy, science, psychology, and art, with the spirit and curiosity of a pioneer and entrepreneur. Like Rowan, he is ultimately a practical doer.

Knowledge is power, but doing empowers.

The Blue-Collar Scholar is not after perfection. His focus is on the 80 percent solution, so that he can start taking action now! This approach includes a personal growth mindset and an openness to learn and evolve.

STICKS

A Blue-Collar Scholar becomes the expert at being an expert by using a simple system I call "STICKS":

- Situation

- Toss aside beliefs

- Immersion

- Conscious, competent learner

- Kick out what's not useful

- State of mind

You must see your current situation clearly, and be able to toss aside beliefs in order to grow and change. To become great, you must immerse yourself in what you do, learn as if you are preparing to teach, and kick out what you can't or don't need to use. Finally, you must be in the right state of mind to evolve.

> Discovery consists of seeing what everybody has seen and thinking what nobody has thought.
> —ALBERT VON SZENT-GYORGYI NAGYRAPOLT

ASYMMETRICAL THINKING

Part of the Blue-Collar Scholar approach includes asymmetrical, or out-of-the-box, thinking. SEALs plan and train hard, so that when we are on the mission, we have a sense of déjà vu, a feeling that we've been there before, so it's not as scary. But while we plan and prepare, we want to tap into a sense of "vuja de," of seeing something we've seen countless times before with fresh eyes, as if we're seeing it for the first time, so that we're seeing asymmetrically.

Let's get after it!

THEY WEAR DRESSES, BUT THEY DON'T DANCE

Understanding Fear, Our Greatest Adversary

Bonnie Ware, a palliative care nurse who cared for the terminally ill, wrote *The Top Five Regrets of the Dying*. In the book, she revealed the five most common regrets her patients shared with her on their deathbeds. The number one regret? They wished they had dared to live lives that were true to themselves, not the lives others expected of them. I don't know about you, but I don't want to live a life of regret. I want to live the life that I design, and I most certainly don't want to let my fears get in the way of that.

There is an old adage that says, "Courage is the first of human virtues because it makes all others possible." But before we can be courageous and before we can begin to accomplish all those "other" things, we must first better understand—and learn to manage—fear.

Fear shapes the outcome of our lives, and it is both a gift and a disease. I chose a hazardous profession as a U.S. Navy SEAL. Hell, in some sense, I spent 20 years on my deathbed. Fear keeps us alive if we are being chased by a lion, but in daily life, especially in our work life, a fearful state of mind cripples us. Most experts agree that we are born with only two fears, a fear of falling and a fear of loud noises; the rest is learned. As we grow up, we receive little training on how to deal with fear beyond a few clichés telling us to "face" our fears and "overcome" them. But what does that really mean?

> **Fear keeps us alive if we're being chased by a lion, but in daily life, especially in our work life, fear cripples us.**

If you can't manufacture courage, motivation, and willpower, all the clichés in the world won't help you raise your hand in a board meeting or get off the couch to work out. At least not for more than 90 percent of humans; we all have finite willpower.

OH, DON'T BE LATE FOR THE DANCE

For a 2003 exchange program I was selected as a SEAL Officer to become a member of the British Special Forces. At this time, we were in two major wars, and the British were our most active coalition force, so the strength of our relationship was critical (and still is today). The Special Air Service (SAS) and the Special Boat Service (SBS) produce among the toughest and bravest warriors the world has seen. They conduct covert, clandestine, and direct action missions around the globe. Some say they are fearless, but are they?

I had only been in England for a few months, and I was still getting my bearings and learning the nuances of the culture. One afternoon I was told that the squadron I was in was having a boys' night out, or a "fancy dress" as they call it. I decided to wear a button-up shirt and classic jacket, which I thought was a safe bet.

I arrived at the pub a little early, but not long after, several of the lads rolled in and walked over to me at the bar. At first, I didn't recognize them—they were all wearing *dresses*! I was staring at some of the world's toughest men, who had done some of the most dangerous covert and direct action missions. Not only were they wearing dresses, they had also accessorized with makeup, wigs, and, hell, I believe they even shaved their legs! They looked at me a little strangely and snickered as they realized I hadn't understood the meaning of the "fancy dress" night.

Not too many pints into the evening, we went to a small club. I asked the lads why they were just keeping to themselves at the bar and weren't mingling. The Scotsman who had invited me replied: "Brits don't dance, mate. You won't catch a British man dead on the dance floor. That's for you Yanks."

I was a little confused, but realized it was because they were embarrassed. I pressed him, "So, you wear dresses, but you don't dance?"

"That's right, mate. We don't dance."

In their minds, wearing dresses was so absurd—it was a way to make fun of themselves and have a good laugh. But dancing, which exposes you and makes you a little vulnerable, well, *that* was a bridge too far.

TO FEAR IS HUMAN

Fear has many faces. There are different types of fears, and we all have various levels of immunity to each type. For U.S. Navy SEALs and others in similar professions, physical fear often comes more naturally than others, such as social, moral, and emotional fears. Often what we *think* we fear is not what we really fear, as is the case with public speaking. People often say they feel as if they are going to die before speaking, but what they *really* fear isn't the speaking itself or even the fear of being embarrassed. Rather, it is the fear of feeling incompetent, which could lead to the loss of a job, home, or social standing, in addition to the embarrassment. Fear is complicated.

We know that fear is an unpleasant emotion caused by the *belief* that something is likely to be dangerous and cause pain. Note that fear is a belief, and like any other belief, we can change it. We just need proof, evidence to show us why this belief is no longer valid. Fear is a physical event experienced, not only in the mind, but in the body, and it naturally produces a freeze, fight, or flight response.

Fear is the primary emotion that ensures our survival; it's our survival instinct. It triggers what most people refer to as the "reptile" part of our brain, which happens to be the oldest part. Hundreds of thousands of years ago, humans had predators that preyed on them, and they feared for their personal safety on a daily basis. Our brains are still wired to that level of fear, and our minds naturally look out for danger in our lives. According to researchers roughly 80 percent of our daily thoughts are negative and fear based. Most of those negative thoughts are repetitive, like a movie playing in a loop in our minds. Psychologists use the term *awfulizing*, which means "in a situation of uncertainty, the mind is filled with fear of the worst." Fear replaces the unknown with the awful.

> **When your mind "awfulizes," fear replaces the unknown with the awful.**

Just turn on the news and watch and listen for fear. It's as if humans are obsessed with potential dangers, often overreacting to a perceived threat without rational justification. I believe the 24-hour news cycle has not only created a fearful state of consciousness throughout the United States, it is contributing to national health issues such as depression and anxiety. A horrific event gets played over and over until our minds believe it happens continuously, producing a sense of inevitable doom. If you want to be less fearful, stop watching the news!

> **Fear is a disease. The more you allow it to penetrate your mind, the more it spreads to other parts of your life.**

Threats: Real and Perceived

We know that our fears are mostly irrational, but we have a terrific imagination. Our imagination enables us to paint a picture of something so horrific that it almost can't be spoken about. Some 20 million Americans are reported to have aviophobia, an extreme fear of flying. According to the National Safety Council, Americans have a 1 in 114 chance of dying in a car crash compared to nearly a 1 in 10,000 chance of dying in an aviation accident. These include small planes, private jets, and all the other higher-risk forms of flying. That means you are about 88 times more likely to get killed on the drive to the airport than on the flight. But the mental image of a plane crash is much more vivid, and everyone can imagine the horror that must take place before crashing. Our mind has a great ability to dream up a graphic horror movie of what might happen, even though we know it's unlikely. Now imagine going into combat knowing the threat is very real. It is tangible. The strategies I discuss in this book work no matter what the fear is—real or perceived.

> **The fact that you fear something is evidence that it isn't happening.**

Our minds put perceived threats into context. The amygdala, that reptile part of the brain I mentioned earlier, processes emotions, especially fear. The amygdala speaks to the hippocampus, which speaks to the prefrontal cortex. The hippocampus deals with emotions and long-term memories, while the prefrontal cortex is the executive part of our brain and the newest addition in our evolutionary process. This part gives us the ability to be creative and to control our lives. I will focus on these three areas of the brain when speaking about fear.

Imagine seeing a hungry lion 20 feet away, staring at you. Obviously, that would wake up the reptile part of your brain and put you in survival mode. But imagine seeing that lion through the window of a safari vehicle or in a zoo. The hippocampus and the prefrontal cortex put the threat into context and change our emotional and physical responses. Now imagine being on foot in the Sahara and seeing that hungry lion, but this time you have a high-powered rifle. Even though you would still have fear, being armed gives you a different perspective and puts the situation in a different context. To be clear, I'm not saying we should shoot lions—of course not!—but metaphorically arming yourself is a way of mitigating fear and having a plan.

> **The paradox of evolution**
> **is that our own survival instincts**
> **are killing us.**

Making Fear a Welcome Guest

The way to deal with fear is not to expect to eliminate it altogether. The goal is to mitigate its inappropriate adverse effects and make it a welcome guest, not an intruder of the mind. The "inverted U" curve, created by psychologists Robert Yerkes and John Dodson and published in 1908, describes how pressure and performance increase together until you hit the optimal pressure for a particular task. As pressure continues to increase, performance begins to decline, and eventually, too much stress leads to deficient performance, anxiety, and unhappiness. Too little pressure or stress in life is dull; too much is overwhelming. My GUTS (Greatness Under Tremendous Stress) approach is not about wholly eliminating fear. It's about getting fear into that sweet spot, zone, or flow. It is about managing the stress and channeling it into energy and intent.

> **GUTS is not about eliminating fear; it's about using it to achieve excellence.**

Confidence: The First Line of Defense

Identifying fear in different parts of our lives is critical to understanding the situation (the S in STICKS)—where we are and where we want to go. GUTS will discuss specific techniques to deal with specific fears, some of which are applicable to other parts of your life. Some skills—and the confidence that goes with them—become foundational. For example, people say that martial arts build confidence in people, especially kids. I agree. It's precisely why I've had my son in various forms of martial arts since he was young. Once people have a high level of confidence in their abilities, it tends to flow over to other aspects of their lives.

In the office, we've probably all encountered toxic bullies who can't control their emotions. But bullies are actually insecure and driven by fear. Now consider a person who has been training in martial arts for years, who is very confident in his abilities. Suppose he gets into a heated argument with a toxic bully who is used to having people submit to his demands. We know that a physical confrontation is unlikely to happen in the office, but our reptile brain is still triggered to initiate our survival instincts. Adrenaline kicks in, our heart races, our breathing increases, we get tunnel vision, and the prefrontal cortex (executive brain) shuts down—we can't think clearly. The reptile brain sees and hears the bully's violent cues: loud voice, angry tone, leaning in, pointing, cursing, wide-eyed look, and so forth. But a person highly trained and experienced in martial arts will not get triggered in the same way. His brain will put the situation in a different context. Because he doesn't feel physically threatened, his survival instincts won't kick in, so he can use his executive brain and be rational and clear minded. He may be a little nervous because of social and moral dangers, but he won't shut down in a panic. Instead, he is likely to function effectively in an optimal stress zone—a "sweet spot." The

GUTS process approach is about tactics and techniques to arm ourselves, build confidence, and put fear into the proper situational context to optimize our performance.

> **It's better to be a warrior in a garden**
> **than a gardener in a war.**

Freeze, Fight, or Flight

What happens when we become scared, and why?

It all begins in the amygdala, that small part of our reptile brain, the almond-shaped bundle of neurons that is part of the limbic system. Our focus will be on manipulating this system to our advantage. A stimulus triggers the amygdala, which in turn activates areas involved in the freeze, fight, or flight response. It also triggers the release of stress hormones and activates the sympathetic nervous system.

We all know the feeling of being scared. Our hearts beat faster, we become hyperalert, our mouths turn dry, and our bodies produce adrenaline and cortisol to prepare us for fight or flight. When this happens, our bodies want to move and burn off the cortisol and adrenaline that are being produced.

As a trained tracker, I find it easy to identify the very spot that a person realized she had become lost in the woods. Why do you think that is? Knowing you are lost brings all kinds of horrific images of becoming dehydrated, hungry, and cold; being stalked by predators; and dying in the woods alone. We quickly awfulize the situation, which increases the level of fear. Body reflexes kick in, and the person often begins to run, sometimes back and forth, getting more and more lost. The body wants to move when it's scared. It's designed that way. Once we realize how this works, we can work backward to deal with fear at its source. I will cover this extensively in the chapters that follow.

The Path of Least Resistance

When you learn to track animals and human beings, you learn a great deal about their nature and natural habits. Humans, like other animals, have a natural aversion to straining. Go into the woods, and you will see natural patterns of trails that animals take, even using each other's paths, making the walk more comfortable. Most of the tracks lead to water, food, or a safe place to sleep. Many animals spend most of their time either lying down, standing, or walking, preserving energy until it is needed.

Humans are no different. Physically, intellectually, and emotionally our natural default is the path of least resistance; instinctively, we don't want to strain ourselves. You may disagree, but look at the world we live in for a moment. For instance, when you watch TV, it seems like every commercial is for a new drug that pushes our "easy button"—our desire to take the path of least resistance with no discomfort.

If you ever have trouble sleeping as I have, you've probably seen the late-night infomercials promising the world with virtually no pain. You stand on this board and twist for 15 minutes a day—voila!, you now have a ripped supermodel body. Take this one pill and instantly be skinny, or happy, or whatever it is the infomercials are promising. By offering the path of least resistance, they manipulate our natural human weaknesses.

We have become conditioned to avoid strain and pain and think both should be eliminated from our lives. Our culture is addicted to instant gratification, a culture that attempts to avoid discomfort in all aspects of our lives. The proof? We are the most obese society in the history of the world; nearly 40 percent of Americans fall into this category.[1] The use of antidepressants and other anxiety-relieving drugs is steadily increasing across the nation, and we have an epidemic of taking addicting opioids to relieve physical pain. We are the wealthiest nation in the history of the world, yet we are getting more depressed and have become increasingly fragile. Instant gratification has lowered our threshold for discomfort.[2]

The answer is to avoid the temptation to take the easiest path. And we do this through discipline. Learning to delay gratification and embrace challenges in all areas of our lives will start the process of building discipline.

BRIDGING THE ACCOMPLISHMENT GAP

When I refer to the accomplishment gap, I'm referring to what has become a natural tendency to take the path of least resistance, which, if done repeatedly, will eventually leave us short of our goals and generally feeling "unaccomplished." The gap starts to form when our desire to avoid straining, especially in the face of fear, becomes the dominant factor in most of our decisions to plan or act. We lose the *motivation* to act.

Crossing the gap requires discipline, and discipline forms the bridge that takes us across the accomplishment gap. So how do we build discipline?

The Discipline "Habitude"

You build the foundation of discipline by delaying some form of gratification. It means investing the money instead of spending it, working on the project instead of watching YouTube videos, not checking your phone constantly, not eating that last donut, and so on. Discipline ultimately channels and manufactures motivation. It's a process that creates habits, and more importantly, habits of attitude, which I call "habitudes." Like any habit, it doesn't happen overnight.

> As a "habitude"—a regularly chosen and followed attitude—discipline takes us across the accomplishment gap.

No Easy Way

In the United States, we have an epidemic of stolen valor. The SEALs have an exclusive social media site that almost 2,000 of us use to share information and continue the brotherhood. One of the things we do on this site *daily* is to confront and expose people lying about being a Navy SEAL. Why is that? I've exposed people who were pillars of their communities, frequent guests on TV, prosperous businessmen, family friends, and even a deacon of a church. What would drive someone to do such a thing? People who steal valor want the trophy without the effort of the win. They want the valor of a Navy SEAL without the strain and pain of earning it.

This desire is not uncommon. Most of us have probably fantasized about instantly becoming a master guitarist or speaking a different language, wishing a genie would grant us the skills. But this approach to life fails to bring either success or happiness because much of the happiness, in my experience, is in the straining. I learned this when my first book, *First, Fast, Fearless*, came out. I asked myself, "Now what?" because it turned out that the journey—planning, organizing, and writing the book—was the reward.

Putting Wealth and Success into Perspective

Most people want to achieve their goals and attain success in life. What if you could get into a time machine and fast-forward 10 years into the future when all of your "hard work" has paid off and you've accomplished everything you set out to do? Maybe you had a very successful business or you were rich, famous, or whatever you think you want. If you could fast-forward, would you? Would you skip ahead in life, avoiding the pain and strain of success and go right for the trophy?

Why do many people who win the lottery become unhappy and often claim it ruined their lives? Maybe you're thinking, *I wouldn't be miserable. It would make all of my dreams come true. Those people are idiots.* Or, *Money might not buy happiness, but it sure would make misery more tolerable.*

What value is any trophy in life without the hard work? The greater the work, the more valuable the reward, no matter the trophy. When I see a fellow SEAL wearing his Navy SEAL Trident on his uniform, I know how valuable that is to him, and what it took to get it.

Business tycoon Warren Buffett is one of the richest people in the world, worth billions of dollars. Through his 2006 Buffett Giving Pledge, he has promised to give away 99 percent of his wealth to charity during his lifetime or after death. He has donated a large chunk to the Bill & Melinda Gates Foundation, among other nonprofits. When asked about his decision to give away such wealth instead of leaving it to his children, his response was: "I'll give my children enough money to feel they could do anything, but not so much that they could do nothing." Brilliant, no?

Some people believe Buffett did his children wrong, but he knows that if he gave his children too much wealth, it would have stolen their happiness and ultimately their fulfillment in life. The trophy is meaningless without the struggle and the effort to earn it. The struggle is what brings joy and fulfillment in life. Now intellectually, you're probably nodding with agreement.

But do you *really* believe it? Once you start to believe and feel it, you begin to build a different relationship with struggle and strain, and even fear.

> The elevator to success is out of order,
>
> but the stairs are always open.
>
> —ZIG ZIGLAR

No, none of this happens overnight. I don't have a magic pill, but I do have a proven process. Muscles don't prepare for the last workout; they prepare for future workouts, and over-compensate. That's why you get bigger and stronger when you strain to lift weights. When we strain mentally, emotionally, and physically, those muscles rebound bigger and stronger, preparing for the future. It's a process that builds discipline, motivation, and willpower—first, to deal with fear and then to go beyond and conquer.

> Suffering is the perception of discomfort.

No Pain, No Gain

In Coronado, California, the home of the SEAL Teams, is a large medical facility to treat SEALs and SEAL candidates. The doctors who work there created a cartoon-drawn poster for diagnosing "pain." They found that SEALs reported pain very differently than the normal Navy sailors they were used to treating. While a regular sailor may say "seven" on the pain scale, a SEAL may only report "two." At first, you may think SEALs are just being tough guys, but it's more than that. SEAL training creates a different relationship with discomfort, and SEALs no longer seek to avoid it at all costs because, in our world, discomfort is tied directly to success. In just a few months of basic training, our pain and discomfort tolerances go through the roof. The doctors are the first to point this out. On their poster, they have pictures of various injuries relating to levels of pain, from 1 to 10. A 9 is equivalent to becoming a double amputee; one can only wonder what a 10 is!

GUTS uses all the principles, tools, and experiences of the SEAL world to help you deliberately transform yourselves and your environment to enable you to cross the accomplishment gap.

―――――――― **EXERCISE** ――――――――

Get a pen and paper and write down your "f***-it" list. (I don't use harsh language to be crude; there *is* a purpose. I will explain this further in Chapter 2.) Most people talk about a bucket list, the things they want to do before they die, which I understand and definitely appreciate. But this list is different: it's a list of what you would do if *you weren't consumed by fear.* For me, it was public speaking, improv (comedy), dancing, telling my friends

I love them, and writing this book. Many people fear public speaking more than death, which means they would rather be inside the box than giving the eulogy! Think about that.

Once you have your list, write down beside each item what scares you about it. For me, when it comes to writing a book, my fear is that people will think it's stupid or that I'm dumb. They will see that I have emotional fears and that I'm not the "steely-eyed warrior" they think I am. They may see me as vulnerable.

As soon as you identify and put a name to your fears, they change because you can rationalize and see them for what they are. Next, write down the strain or hurdles that might keep you from getting started. For example, when I started writing *GUTS* I knew that in order to be authentic I had to be vulnerable and say things that I normally would hide. I knew I had to speak about my personal challenges, and I was scared of the ensuing shame or of being judged as not being the person others think I am. When you codify your ideas in a book, you commit, you put yourself out there, and it's scary to know you will be judged publicly, perhaps even harshly. Beyond that, my mind jumped to the hurdles, the straining: I have to get up early, be on the computer for hours at a time to write a proposal, and engage in months of effort and dialogue with my editor to define and sequence the concepts for the chapters before I even start to write the book—all this before dealing with the overwhelming self-doubt that comes with the process of writing itself. The list can go on and on, can't it?

Write your hurdles down and keep the list to yourself for now. We will come back to it later.

TAKEAWAYS

- Fear is the main obstacle to accomplishing our goals in business and in life.

- Fear is not all bad; it's our survival instinct.

- What we *think* we fear may not be what we *really* fear.

- Eighty percent of our daily thoughts are negative and fear based.

- The mind has a tendency to replace the unknown with fear, a process known as "awfulizing."

- The "reptile brain," or amygdala, governs your first response to fear, which may be rational or irrational: freeze, fight, or flight.

- Confidence is the first line of defense in dealing with fear.

- Avoidance of strain or discomfort ("the path of least resistance") works hand in hand with fear to create the "accomplishment gap," the gap between where you are and where you want to be in business and in life.

- A "habitude" is an attitude that becomes a habit (e.g., not checking your phone every minute so you can pay proper attention to the people around you). This reflects an attitude (prioritizing attention to others) and the discipline to make it a habit. A good set of habitudes will transform you.

- As used by SEALs in combat, GUTS applies a systematic understanding and mitigation of fear, discipline, motivation, and willpower to get you across the gap—whether it be onto the dance floor in a dress, through an executive presentation at work, or past a difficult discussion at home—to the life you design for yourself.

2

IT'S YOUR GUT

Taking Extreme Ownership
of the Outcome

When candidates show up to SEAL Training, we start to control the language they use to establish the mental framework and discipline to be a SEAL. SEALs conduct our nation's most strategic missions; often they are "no-fail" missions that affect national security. When a SEAL student is asked whether he completed his mission, there are three possible responses: "Yes," "No," and "I f***ed up!"

Saying "I f***ed up" is a form of ownership because you own the outcome and are not excusing yourself by blaming something or someone other than you. Saying it out loud is an important component, even if the students are thinking of excuses at the time. There may be circumstances out of their control that keep them from completing the mission. We know that, but the goal here is to hammer home that they will not be excused for failing to complete the mission because they own the outcome. It breaks the cycle of excuses and forces students to be innovative, creating an invisible force that compels them to accomplish what they intend to do. This drives teamwork, self-reliance, and a can-do and will-do attitude. Out of necessity, they start to solve their problems in very creative ways.

Language matters, and the words we choose develop our thoughts and make them clearer. Those thoughts become actions, and our actions eventually make us who we are.

TIME OUT: A BRIEF WORD
ABOUT LANGUAGE

One day my nine-year-old son and I were in the house playing with some of his Star Wars toys. He stopped what he was doing and looked at me. I could tell he wanted to ask a question, so I stopped what I was doing and looked back at him. He said, "Daddy, I bet you cursed a lot in combat, didn't you?" He had a look of thoughtful curiosity in his eyes, and I knew he'd been thinking about this for some time. I'm not a saint, but my wife and I do try to control our language in the house, and as much as humanly possible in the car, but we know how difficult that can be at times. Obviously, I'm worse than she is, having spent most of my adult life in the Navy.

Our day-to-day language comes from the left hemisphere of our brain, the cerebral cortex, which is associated with our higher thought processes. But cursing comes from our older reptile brain, the amygdala, in the limbic system in the brain's right hemisphere. Cursing is connected to strong emotions such as anger, lust, fear, and even compassion. Curse words are so emotionally powerful in our society that many have been banned from TV, books, and games; some are also outlawed or considered hate crimes in certain contexts. Words are powerful.

A 2017 *New Yorker* magazine article by Melissa Mohr, the author of *Holy Sh*t: A Brief History of Swearing*, cites an interesting study. In 2009, Richard Stephens, a psychologist at Keele University in England, asked a group of volunteers to plunge one hand into a bucket of ice-cold water and keep it there for as long as they could. Stephens sometimes instructed them to utter an expletive of their choice—one that "they might use if they banged their head or hit their thumb with a hammer," according to an article he wrote about the study. Other times he had them utter a neutral word, like "wooden" or "brown." With few exceptions, the volunteers could hold their hands in the water for longer when they cursed—about 40 seconds longer, on average. Stephens believed swearing to be a form of pain management and empowerment and went on to do other studies to prove it.

In the *New Yorker* article, Mohr also refers to a 2011 study at the University of Bristol that found that saying swear words prompted an emotional reaction in the people who said them, and researchers could detect an increase in the conductivity of their skin. These studies show, in fact, that the use of strong language can both get you charged up and create a physical reaction that helps you better deal with pain.

The bottom line: Cursing and taboo words trigger the oldest part of our brains, and they can be powerful and useful when used correctly and sparingly as a tool to get things done.

ACCOUNTABILITY: OWNERSHIP
TO THE EXTREME

Accountability is the *extreme ownership* of an outcome. In a dangerous profession, you must understand that the result often happens *to* you. It's not something that you observe; it becomes part of you. To understand extreme ownership, you must first believe that we all have free will and can make choices with that free will. Personal accountability is a choice, yet it is also a fact of life. What you choose is what your life turns into; it happens to you.

Accountability Means No Excuses

We give SEAL candidates more tasks than they can complete, and we give them timelines to force them to prioritize and think in asymmetrical ways to accomplish the mission. I know it seems a little harsh, and maybe unfair, that we treat students this way knowing we induce failure, but allowing no excuses serves the goal of breaking the relationship most people have with excuses and with failure. Making excuses wastes mental energy and time hunting for something or someone to blame for failures. It can also affect our belief in our own performance. By not allowing excuses, we demand greater effort from students. Over time, this fosters innovation and all-in commitment. And this individual all-in commitment amplified many times over in teams results in an invisible force capable of achieving the most challenging of missions. The whole becomes greater than the sum of its parts.

In the SEAL Teams, leaders can and have been fired, even though they were not directly responsible for a misstep made by their teams. It doesn't happen often, but it does happen. As I write this book, a SEAL platoon was sent home from deployment for misconduct; when they came back, the senior leaders were fired, and their careers basically ended. They weren't present overseas when the misconduct happened, *yet they were accountable*. It is important to understand that standards become what leaders allow.

Accountability Cannot Be Outsourced

One of my pet peeves is watching people cross a road in front of a stop sign while not paying any attention to oncoming traffic, assuming everyone will actually stop. I say this because I watched a 20-something-year-old man texting while walking through the crosswalk, never diverting his attention to a 4,000-pound vehicle coming his way. The driver of the car slowed down enough to make a right turn but did not come close to stopping. He hit the man at significant speed. The man flew over the driver's side of the car, landing just on the other side of the driver's door. I ran to the injured man to assess his injuries; they weren't fatal, but they weren't good. His leg was broken and probably his knee as well. Whose fault was it? Or should I say, who was to blame? Does it matter? The young man will most likely spend the rest of his life dealing with those injuries—the outcome happened to him.

Of course, the driver will be held responsible. His insurance will probably go up a few hundred dollars a year, but the man on the ground will deal with this for the rest of his life. He owns the outcome; he is accountable for his life. Yes, the driver should have stopped, but the man who got hit had outsourced his safety. Yes, the injured man is in the right, but how does that help him?

> **Accountability in life cannot be delegated;**
>
> **your life is your own.**

Accountability Means Accepting Our Own Failures

The man who was hit had outsourced the outcome of his life to someone or something other than himself. As a society, we often rely on a higher authority—parents, spouses, bosses, law enforcement, teachers, politicians, "experts with certificates and licenses," etc.—to decide the outcome of our lives. GUTS accountability is about choosing to accept ownership of your life and not outsourcing it to anyone or anything else. The Blue-Collar Scholar takes from the experts what she can use, but kicks out what is not useful. She owns herself.

Accountability Implies an Enduring Relationship

Ownership of something has an extreme and profound impact on the relationship we have with it. I use the word "relationship" because, just like any relationship, you need to work continually on it, be deliberate about it, and, in a way, fall in love with it.

Dan Gilbert, a professor of psychology at Harvard University, did a study on anterograde amnesia, a rare condition that makes it impossible for a person to acquire new memories. In his research, he presented individuals with this condition with six paintings and asked them to rank them from the one they liked best to the one they liked least. He told them they would receive a poster of one of the paintings they had chosen, but instead of their favorite, they could choose between their third and fourth picks. The individuals chose their third best-liked painting. He then left the room, waited a sufficient amount of time, and returned. By then the subjects had not only forgotten the experiment, they had even forgotten who he was, so he explained the process again. When Gilbert asked them to rank their six paintings, their choices had changed.

Now one would think that since the participants had no memory of the experiment, they would predictably put the paintings in the same order. But that is not what happened. They actually ranked their third pick second and their fourth pick fifth. Remember that Gilbert had promised to give the participants a poster of their third pick. Although none of them remembered the experiment, somehow, something was triggered in their minds that made them think they owned that poster and therefore they liked it better! The poster they rejected the first time, their fourth pick, they ranked lower and liked less because they had already rejected it.

Accountability Means Ending the Blame Game

When we *choose* to own something, we can fall in love with it. When we choose to take extreme ownership of the outcomes of our lives, we can then fall in love with our lives and stop blaming and finger-pointing to find who's at fault for failures. That frees us from our past and gives us ownership of our future.

I'm sure you've had coworkers and managers (and family members, for that matter) who contribute little to a discussion or outcome, but strive to "find the fault" in anything someone else does or says. It's the easy way out. Rather than doing the hard work themselves and being fully accountable for the organization's success, they try to look and act important or smart by finding the faults or weaknesses in the work of others. For many, it becomes the *only* thing they do day in, day out. Playing "find the fault" may look smart, but it means they do not own the trajectory of their lives. They have outsourced their lives to someone or something else; they are not *accountable*. They look back and excuse themselves with the past. They don't care about or love the outcome in a way that gives them ownership of their futures.

> **Accountability is both freedom from the past and ownership of the present and future.**

Accountability Means Investing in the Outcome

When we outsource the results in our lives or focus on the excuses, we never fully accept ownership and, therefore, never wholly invest ourselves in the outcome. As a result, we never love our lives the way we can. Excuses feel good, but they don't *do* good, so it's best to sever that relationship with excuses and own the outcome. Don't get me wrong, SEALs still have the desire to excuse themselves just like anyone else; however, we are conditioned to be aware of it and don't allow it in our organization. For instance, we often do "monster mashes," major physical fitness events that challenge and push our fitness levels and that can last almost all day. When we're all standing around about to start the evolution, it's not uncommon for some to start making excuses for why they won't perform at their best: "Oh man, I did a huge run yesterday," "I pulled a muscle in my leg recently," "I've been out of town for a month," and so on.

We say, "Go ahead and put that shit in the excuse locker and leave it there!" An "excuse locker" looks a lot like a trash can because that's what it really is. We laugh at each other and make fun of those who fill the excuse locker the most. But we get it out of our system, and yes, it does feel good. But making excuses up front is like justifying losing before the game even begins; it's failing before starting. If you leave them behind in the excuse locker, that's OK—just never mention them again.

A few years ago, I worked with legendary baseball player and pitching coach Rick Peterson to help him develop his book *Crunch Time: How to Be Your Best When It Matters Most*. He was the pitching coach during the "Moneyball" era with the Oakland A's, a saga told in a bestselling book and very successful movie. We had long discussions about some of his best pitchers and what made them successful. I told him about the excuse locker concept and how SEAL training breaks the relationship with excuses and teaches ownership of the outcome. I compared baseball with a SEAL deployment. Major League teams play 162 games a year; during a typical deployment into combat a SEAL team conducts that many or more missions in a six-month period. It's not like the movies; it's a grind, physically and emotionally. You have to get up every day and focus on being your best when you don't feel your best. Near the end of a deployment, you may have broken fingers, twisted and swollen joints, stitches, a few concussions from blasts, a painful back, all while being physically and emotionally exhausted—but your enemy doesn't care that you're not feeling your best. It dawned on Rick that his best pitchers didn't focus on their small injuries. They learned to play at their best when they didn't feel their best. They left their excuses in the locker room and didn't dwell on them during the game.

> **Break your relationship with excuses**
>
> **and own the outcome.**

Outsourcing our lives makes us fragile. Even our happiness becomes dependent on something or someone else, not ourselves. I know this all too well. For years, I was "working" on a book with a family member who was a trained "writer" and was responsible for the writing. And for years nothing got done. I felt helpless and hopeless because neither he nor I held him accountable for deadlines and doing the work. Six months turned into six years. Outsourcing made me feel like a prisoner, helpless to accomplish a goal I'd set. I didn't feel like I owned my own future; *responsibility can be delegated, but accountability cannot.* Eventually, I held him accountable and fired him. I took back ownership of the writing outcome. A little more than a year later, I had an agent, a contract with McGraw Hill, and a bestselling book.

In the SEAL Teams, we are quick to learn that although we operate with overlapping fields of accountability, you are accountable for your own life. No one cares about it as much as you do, so take care of it.

> **Outsourcing our lives makes us fragile and dependent on others.**

THE DIFFERENCE BETWEEN ORGANIZATION AND ORGANISM

It is blatantly obvious when an organization lacks accountability. Promises are made, yet there is little evidence of consequences for or ownership of the outcome by those who break those promises.

When I speak to teams about overlapping accountability, I use the metaphor of an *organism*, not an organization. Organizations often have silos, different departments with conflicting goals that are almost always full of excuses and finger-pointing. When you operate as an *organism*, you operate knowing that failures and mistakes happen to everyone on the *team*; small businesses and aviation crews understand that if they go down, they all go down together.

> An organization confines responsibility to individual silos and shows little accountability for the total outcome. An organism features overlapping accountabilities, minimizing mistakes and maintaining focus on the total outcome. Everyone has ownership of that outcome.

The more an organization acts like an organism, the better.

DIRECT RESPONSIBILITY, CHOSEN RESPONSIBILITY, AND SELF-LEADERSHIP

The responsibility I refer to is a sense of personal responsibility as a human being and leader that I choose to accept. It goes above and beyond the responsibility I'm given. Although I'm retired from the SEAL Teams, I still consider myself a steward of society, and when I'm around, I want people to feel safer, better off, and happier because I'm in the room. When that 20-something-year-old man was hit by the car at the stop sign,

I didn't wait for someone else to act. And I sure as hell never thought it wasn't my responsibility to get involved.

In life and in every organization (not an organism), the bystander effect is widespread. This effect often occurs in the presence of others, especially in an emergency situation, like the young man being hit. The more people are present, the more likely each person will defer the implied responsibility of helping and assume it's someone else's issue to deal with. The self-leadership I advocate implies a sense of overall personal responsibility.

In the workplace, the bystander effect, or lack of personal responsibility, keeps people from addressing problems that are often elephants in the room. People frequently allow bullying, discrimination, toxic behavior, and, as we've seen recently with the #metoo movement, sexual harassment in the workplace. Remember, as a leader, what you tolerate becomes the new standard. So instead of focusing on who *else* is responsible, focus on building a strong sense of personal responsibility. If you see something that needs to be done, do it or take responsibility. That's genuine accountability and evidence of true self-leadership. It's also the kind of leadership that holds others accountable and develops a sense of personal responsibility in team members for the greater good of all, enabling the team to operate like an organism.

> **If not me, then who? If not now, when?**
>
> **—HILLEL THE ELDER**

EXERCISE

Write down the three responses on a sticky note and put it where you will see it often. When you catch yourself responding to others and even yourself with anything other than "Yes," "No," or "I f***ed up," ask yourself why you are doing so. When you stick (or return) to these three answers, it will start to break your relationship with excuses and build a stronger sense of accountability. As you do this, you will become increasingly conscious of the excuses you make, and you'll gain an appreciation for how frequently most people excuse themselves for their failures. Remember, excuses *feel* good but don't *do* good.

TAKEAWAYS

- Accountability is the extreme ownership of an outcome.

- When accountable, the only answers are "Yes," "No," and "I f***ed up."

- Accountability means no excuses.

- Accountability cannot be outsourced.

- Accountability means accepting our own failures.

- Accountability means accepting the failures of others and acting for the common good. Playing the blame game with other team members accomplishes little.

- *Not* being accountable makes us fragile, fearful, tentative, and dependent on others.

- *Being* accountable frees us from the past and gives us ownership of the future.

- Organizations operate in silos, with narrow responsibilities but little accountability for common results. An organism has overlapping accountabilities in which everyone has ownership of the outcome.

- Excuses *feel* good but don't *do* good.

3

ON THE "X"

Using Live Ammo and Brutal Honesty to Achieve Excellence

L ate one night in Iraq in 2007, one of our SEAL Chiefs was
leading a mission to hunt down high-level Al-Qaeda terrorists with SEALs and Iraqis in Anbar province. The goal was
to clear the structure and capture or kill the enemy combatants.
The Chief made entry into the building, and from 15 feet away,
he was engaged by four heavily armed terrorists; the SEAL behind him was killed instantly. The Chief's rifle was shot and destroyed, but his training kicked in, so he drew his pistol and
engaged the enemy. He was shot 27 times (yes, 27 times!), 11
in his armor and 16 in his body, but he didn't quit. He killed
all four enemy fighters with a handgun, all while being shot at
point-blank range.

Is this Chief a superman? No, he's a well-trained SEAL who
went through intensive Close Quarters Battle (CQB) training,

during which SEALs use live ammunition and plastic marking rounds (simunition). In training using simunition, it's very
common to go into a room in which the opposing force is waiting and starts firing at you as you enter. The instructor cadre will
immediately yell, "Fight, fight, fight, fight. Win the fight. Keep
shooting!" Even though you are feeling the pain of those plastic
bullets, you must not stop fighting, you must continue until you
win. Of course, we know that we might not live long enough in
combat to win, but we train for it, so when the time comes, we
react like the Chief. If you're not dead, you're still fighting. The
Chief fell back on his training during this worst-case scenario,
and he won. Maybe the Chief is a superman because after that,
he walked himself to the helicopter for evacuation.

What is so special about SEAL training? What is it about
SEAL training that enabled the Chief to overcome his fear and
fight on against such odds? As you'll see, SEALs are trained
using scenarios as close to combat as possible to inoculate us
against fear and to practice winning during the worst of times.

WHAT IS THE "X"?

The "X" is the spot of contact with the enemy. When you are on
the "X," you need to be at your best. Being on the "X" teaches
you just how prepared or unprepared you are. In all phases of
our training we focus on getting as close as possible to the "X,"
so that when we find ourselves in tough and critical situations,
we are as prepared as we can be.

LIVE AMMO

In every phase of training throughout our SEAL careers, we use live ammunition and explosives, as well as simunition fired from real weapons, to get as close to the "X" and combat reality as possible. We use live ammunition against static targets and simunition against other SEALs. These plastic rounds are designed to mark the impact of a bullet. Although they're not lethal, they do pack a sting. During CQB training, we switch back and forth from live ammo to simunition. Firing live rounds in close proximity to each other and going head-to-head against each other dials up the stress factor significantly and gives us a real feel of the fight, enabling us to train as close to the "X" as possible.

The use of live ammunition creates a training environment unlike any other. Once you lock and load a live bullet, the mindset shifts; the reality of the situation demands complete focus and honesty.

When I use the terms "live ammo" and "close to the 'X'" in this book, I refer to the strategy of putting yourself into situations as real as possible that force you to be honest and compel you to evolve. *Doing* reveals hidden truths that studying and theory cannot give you. When you use live ammo close to the "X," you experience uncertainty, fear, and danger, and you develop the intuition to deal with them under fire.

Like every strategy in this book, live ammo forces you to be honest and enables you to achieve excellence in the most challenging situations. You'll be better prepared, more confident and aware, and better able to respond to the events happening around you. How do you use live ammo at your job? Accept a difficult assignment, a critical project with high stakes, something close to the "X" for the entire organization. Make the tough calls and take initiative and responsibility, even if you're not given enough resources to carry out the assignment. Teach your team members your leadership philosophy. Why is this so important? Because teaching forces us to be honest, shows us what we do and don't know, and requires us to commit to what we actually believe while reinforcing those beliefs with action.

BLOWING THE DOORS OFF: DIRECT ACTION ASSAULTS

Direct action assaults are one of the most common and most important SEAL missions. Direct action assaults involve a team of as many as 40 SEALs who breach an entry point into a building or ship to engage the enemy at close range in CQB. The enemy doors are often heavily secured, so the breaching is usually done with explosives, as manual breaching wouldn't work. The training for this mission is time-consuming, exhausting, and very dangerous. We use what we call "kill houses," large structures designed for shooting with live ammunition to simulate and get as close as possible to a combat environment, the "X." Additionally, we use concussion grenades, a grenade designed to stun people in the room but not harm them. This training is extremely dangerous and requires a lot of focus and coordination. I've been involved in two major accidents during this training in which one SEAL was paralyzed and the other was killed. In our profession, training safety is important but not the paramount consideration. If safety were paramount, we wouldn't train with live ammo, nor would we jump out of planes at night loaded down with 200 pounds of equipment from 30,000 feet in the sky.

Every time we retrain in Close Quarters Battle, we cover the basics of the crawl, walk, run theory: we start slow and progress to live rounds and explosives. Once the live bullets start flying, you can feel the difference in the training. The focus level increases as the level of anxiety increases. If someone loses situational awareness of exactly where he is in relation to the others on his team, he can get hurt, or even worse, hurt one of his teammates.

In all of our training, our philosophy is "train like you fight, because you will inevitably fight like you train." This concept pervades every aspect of our organization. When the stress dial gets turned up, you don't rise to the occasion, you fall back on your level of training. During times of stress, you need to act without thinking. Your training is what saves you. We train for the worst-case scenario so that we react in a way that wins the fight.

> **Train like you fight; fight like you train.**

Miyamoto Musashi was Japan's most celebrated swordsman. Throughout his life, he killed more than 60 men in armed combat, in fights to the death. In his *Book of Five Rings*, written at the end of his long career as a warrior, he describes the importance of training like you fight. "It is essential that you understand there is no difference between using the sword in combat and in practice. There is no such thing as a grip for striking and a grip for practice."

NO QUITTING ON THE "X"

You may not be risking your life when you go to work, but you do face metaphorical bullets every day. If you put yourself as close to the "X" as possible by using live ammo, no matter what the situation, you'll do better when the going gets tough. Here are a couple of examples: If you are going to give a big sales presentation to a very important potential new client, the first shots fired at you should *not* be during the presentation. Just as attorneys prepare their witnesses for trial by subjecting them to relentless and aggressive questioning, you should prepare by doing a mock presentation to critical naysayers you've tasked to shoot holes into everything you say, so that you don't freeze in fear when those shots come during the actual event. Don't practice stopping and starting over during the mock presentation, keep going—just like the Chief never practiced quitting.

As a SEAL leader, negative performance counseling is one of the most stressful and important things we do. Performance reviews, especially to direct reports who are underperforming, can be challenging, but they are a highly beneficial tool to help people grow. However, if not executed well, they can lead to future hostility and resentment. Don't leave it to chance. Do a mock review and ask someone you trust to play the role of the problematic employee, shooting live ammunition at you, so you get as close to the "X" as possible before you conduct the review.

Learn to speak to top leadership by *doing* it. Take on hard assignments by volunteering for them. Put yourself as close to the "X" as often as you can, and when the chips are down and you're under fire, you'll inevitably perform optimally.

COMPETENCE, NOT ARROGANCE

SEALs are responsible for the nation's most critical missions, and we don't plan to fail; every mission is a no-fail mission. We push ourselves in training to find out exactly where we stand, and this creates honesty and, more importantly, humility. In a VUCA (volatility, uncertainty, complexity, ambiguity) environment, humility opens the door to understanding, to learning and evolving, to continuous improvement. Ego shuts this door to preserve a distorted self-image.

In social psychology, the Dunning-Kruger effect is a theory that people overestimate their own competence; they have cognitive bias. In 1999, psychologists David Dunning and Justin Kruger tested participants in grammar, logic, and humor. After the test, they interviewed the students to ask them about their perceived abilities in each of the fields tested. The students who performed way below average on the tests believed they were well above average in those areas, while the students who scored the highest underestimated their abilities because they thought the test was easy, so they assumed it was easy for everyone. The danger zone is arrogant unconscious incompetence because we believe we are competent, but we aren't, and our arrogance stops us from learning.

Almost 90 percent of people believe they are above average drivers, nearly 95 percent of college professors think they're better than their colleagues.[1] How can that be? It seems the less you know, the more you *think* you know, and the more you know, the more you know you don't know. As Charles Darwin once said, "Ignorance more frequently begets confidence than does knowledge: It is those who know little, and not those who know much, who so positively assert that this or that problem will never be solved by science."[2]

The Blue-Collar Scholar approach to improving and learning is to step as close to the "X" as you can with a humble conscious incompetence mindset—knowing that you do not know—as a starting point. And when I refer to the "X," I mean situations that carry real risk that will force you to change and grow. Nothing is more honest than a live bullet, and any highly successful organization needs to use brutal honesty to strive for excellence. Brutal honesty is a form of live ammunition.

> On the "X," conscious incompetence becomes unconscious competence.

BAPTISM BY FIRE

The truth is, we all lie to ourselves. Or, to put it more generously, we deceive ourselves and hide from reality. Walk into a gym, and you'll notice a guy hitting a speed bag so rapidly that it looks like a fan blade, so fast you can't even see it. But once this guy steps into the ring and gets punched in the face, everything changes. The speed bag doesn't hit back, but on the "X," the other fighter does. If he spars regularly and gets punched in the face enough times, then he will know what to do because he has learned how to deal with it. The feeling you have when you get punched in the face for the first time cannot be taught; it can only be learned. As SEALs, we train as hard as we can, but the first time you get shot at—"baptism by fire"—it teaches you nuances that you would not have otherwise known. The deeper and more frequently you train with live ammo, the less fear you will have in the future when you get on the "X." You'll have experience close to the "X" under live fire.

> The feeling you have when you get punched in the face for the first time cannot be taught; it can only be learned.

Growing up I was fascinated by Arnold Schwarzenegger. I started to pump iron like him. I couldn't get enough of his determination to be a champion. I give him a lot of credit for my success and ultimately earning a Division One college baseball scholarship.

During his ascent to the top of the bodybuilding world, Arnold noticed that, despite his well-developed upper body, his calves were small and unimpressive. Yet even he could not find the motivation to work on his calf muscles. In his book *Encyclopedia of Modern Bodybuilding*, he includes a picture from his late teens, showing him posing in water deep enough to cover his calves. When he noticed this weakness and realized that he could not solve the fault by himself, he forced himself to use live ammo. As he explains:

The first thing I did was to cut off the bottoms of my training pants. Now my calves were exposed for me and everyone else to see. If they were underdeveloped— and they were—there was no hiding the fact. And the only way I could change the situation was to train my calves so hard and so intensely that the back of my legs would come to resemble huge boulders. At first, this was embarrassing. The other bodybuilders in the gym could see my weakness, and they consistently made comments. But the plan eventually paid off. No longer able to ignore my calves, I was determined to build them into one of my best body parts. Psychologically, it was a brutal way to accomplish this, but it worked, and that is what I really cared about. When I stepped on stage at a competition two years after I first began trying so hard to bring up my calves, and I turned my back to the audience, my calves were so huge that I got an ovation even before I flexed them.

Finding the "X" in life is to expose your weaknesses so that you can work on them. It forces you to be honest.

What does this mean to you and how can it work for you? Your task is to find your own live ammo in the areas in which you wish to achieve something, and then to be honest and figure out under what conditions you will improve the most. For instance, when I wanted to lose a few extra pounds, I didn't avoid the beach, I went to the beach and took my shirt off, and I got a scale that measured body fat percentage. I did what Arnold did. I put myself in a position that forced me to confront my goals, and it worked.

MAKING USE OF LIVE AMMO

In planning for the publication of *First, Fast, Fearless,* I began preparing to speak professionally. In the SEAL Teams, I was regularly in front of groups, having given briefs on hundreds of missions and strategic analyses to hundreds of people. My confidence was reasonably high, but I knew that speaking in front of military personnel wasn't the same as speaking in front of business leaders. When I'm giving a mission brief, I'm not exactly interested in connecting emotionally with the audience. It's all about providing information about the mission, while showing nothing other than courage and confidence. I don't have to gain their attention—the situation does it for me.

I wanted to get better on the "X," so I used live ammo by finding local groups and volunteering to speak at events whenever I could. It didn't take long for me to realize how much I didn't know and how much I needed to learn. It was painful. I had an issue with vulnerability. I didn't want to open up in front of people, so I was terrible at connecting with an audience. As a consequence, I spoke like a robot. Honestly, I was quite dull. But I kept speaking in front of small groups until I started to find my rhythm and grew comfortable with being myself on stage, which was not easy to do. I also did improv (comedy) classes to really put myself out there and to experience new things. Practicing in front of a mirror is excellent and helpful, but once you get on stage and the fear and vulnerability kick in, and you see the faces in the crowd—most are staring at you, but some are on their phones or may even be nodding off—you learn what the mirror can't teach. I am building my skills with each event, figuring out what went well and what I can do better. I haven't mastered it *yet*, but I am working on it. It's a process.

Developing this skill has transformed me in ways that I didn't foresee. I've been on dozens of national and local news shows, I did a History Channel series, and I've been asked to host future shows by two production companies. None of this would have happened had I not used live ammo. I didn't start off by speaking to 2,000 people at a national conference. I started out by talking to small groups that I knew wouldn't be hostile, so that the experience wouldn't be terrifying. I started small and slowly went bigger; along the way I built my competence and inoculated myself against fear. A little live ammo goes a long way.

If there is one skill that I would recommend, it's to train in public speaking. Get in front of people, and learn to tell stories that connect with the audience. Leaders and self-leaders must be excellent communicators, and the best way to get there is to use live ammo.

I realize that using live ammo—whatever it may be for you—dials up the fear and doubt. It requires motivation. It may be daunting, but if you use live ammo and are ruthlessly honest about it—and yourself—you will reap rewards you never imagined possible.

EXERCISE

Look at the areas in your life that are important to you and see how you can use live ammunition in those areas to force improvements. For example, if you are a leader, lock and load a 360-degree evaluation to find out how you lead. Work on self-improvement. Begin by telling your team what you are working on, and ask them to hold you accountable whenever you fall back on bad habits or unproductive behavior. Demand brutal honesty; it drives excellence.

TAKEAWAYS

- Train like you fight, and fight like you train. There is no substitute for *doing*.

- Using live ammo close to the "X" is the strategy of putting yourself into situations as real as possible that force you to be honest and compel you to evolve.

- There is no quitting once you're on the "X."

- On the "X," you evolve from conscious incompetence to unconscious competence.

- The "X" starts as a learning tool and becomes a platform for transformation.

- Brutal honesty is a trait that drives excellence.

4

ALWAYS READY

Achieving and Maintaining a
State of Front Sight Focus

Before heading off to Afghanistan, knowing I would be driving around in clandestine vehicles with another Special Forces soldier, I went to and trained at a professional race car driving school. At the end of the first lecture, before heading out to the track, the instructor concluded with an important point: "By the way, don't stare at the wall." One of the best race car drivers of all time, Mario Andretti, gave the same advice when asked about his secret for becoming a world-class champion. He said the direction you focus on is the direction you will follow, and if you stare at the wall, you will probably hit it.

> **The direction you focus on is the direction you will follow.**
>
> **Don't look where you don't want to go.**

FRONT SIGHT FOCUS

In the world of warfare, you want to become the best shooter possible. You want the weapon to be an extension of your arm, and you want to be able to feel it and be sensitive to its nuances. Only a few points of performance are required to be a great shooter, but you must master them to be at a world-class level. Our secondary weapon (behind the M4 rifle, our primary weapon) is the pistol, one of the most difficult weapons to master. Small mistakes, even at close targets, become exaggerated due to the short sight radius between a pistol's back and front sight posts for aiming. For decades my technique for firing a pistol was to repeat in my mind and often out loud, "Front sight, front sight, front sight." I did this thousands of times during my career.

This technique reminds and forces me to focus my eye on the front sight of the weapon so that it is crystal clear, rather than focus on the target I'm aiming at; the target will be blurry. People with no shooting experience will think this is strange, but if you focus on the target instead of the front sight, you will miss. Your eye can focus on only one distance at a time, so it is the front sight post that must be in focus and clear. Being able to control your focus is a necessary skill for any type of success in our lives.

As a SEAL officer instructor running Hell Week for our Basic Underwater Demolition/SEAL (BUD/S) training programs, I did quick counseling sessions with the students when they quit the program to make sure I captured the "why," but also to make sure the students were being honest with themselves. I would get excuses like "I saw God" or "I don't want to hurt people," but I kept pushing because they needed to be honest about why they had quit. We also needed to learn those reasons so that we could improve our mental training program. Quickly they would 'fess up that they were cold and miserable, and simply couldn't do this training for 20 more weeks.

The students lost their focus on the moment, allowing their attention to shift. They looked into the future and saw the distance between themselves and the target. The reality: the students didn't *have to* do this for 20 more weeks; all they had to do was another second, another minute, another hour. They worried that they couldn't continue this type of rigorous training, and that worry was nothing but predicting failure and pain in the future.

Ninety Percent of Success Is Showing Up

The type of training and level of discomfort involved requires you to be in the moment and to maintain your focus on the present, not the future. Each student I went through BUD/S with just wanted to make it to the sixth week—Hell Week, a six-day intensive training regimen on a four-hour *per week* sleep maximum. Our "long-term" focus was on starting Hell Week; we didn't look down the road any further.

In writing this book my focus was not to sit down for eight hours a day and write; my goal was to start! My offensive focus was on getting my hands on the computer. After a few hours, I'd start to discover my ideas and my voice. At that point, I wouldn't stop because I knew that it would be a long way back to where I'd left off if I did. But the key to it all was getting to the starting line with my fingers on the keyboard.

Many people talk about wanting to write a book. I consider that an empty goal; the real goal is to *become a writer*. Being a writer is about patience, motivation, and discipline—and about showing up ready to roll when it's time to write. It has been said that 90 percent of life is just showing up. That applies to *success* as well.

Focus Discipline

In the SEAL Teams, we use extreme discipline when carrying any weapon. Having "muzzle discipline"—knowing at all times where the muzzle is pointing—is paramount. For weeks before students even fire a gun, they carry an empty one. They are watched like a hawk to make sure their muzzle never crosses the path of something they do not wish to destroy. Analogous to this "muzzle discipline," *focus discipline* in the SEAL Teams is absolutely critical to mission success.

The world is full of "focus thieves" that compete for our attention—pop-up ads, commercials, texts, email and news notifications; multiple tasks; and thousands of others. We have increasingly shorter attention spans and attention deficit disorder is on the rise. You can imagine the number of focus thieves that may be operating in a combat arena, yet those pale in comparison to the focus thieves lurking in civilian life!

We all know how it feels to be talking with people who are addicted to their phones. We barely command any of their attention; it's absolutely annoying and sad. I see parents glued to their phones while they "watch" their child score a soccer goal or get a hit in baseball. The parents may be there, but they are not *present* and don't really experience it. The inability to maintain focus has created a population of people who can do things that require limited attention but can't master anything. They become *transactional*, not *transformational* in their lives. Transactional people can't transform an organization, much less themselves.

> **Without focus, we become transactional, not transformational, individuals.**

It's not hard to imagine how being transactional and constantly distracted by the latest stimuli can undermine transformational performance in the workplace, at home, or anywhere else you're trying to achieve something important. Effective self-leadership to achieve transformational goals—to bridge the accomplishment gap—requires a steadier, clearer, more intense focus on your goals and your means to achieve them. Sure, in combat situations, as well as at work and at home, you

need to respond to some of the stimuli present, or else you become insensitive to counter movements, competition, and
change. But you won't accomplish a thing if you change *only* in
response to the latest stimuli and lose sight of your goals in the
process.

"ALL-IN" TRAINING

In the SEAL Teams, we used to debate about whether to travel
to train. We were deploying around the world regularly, so we
tried to eliminate as much travel to train as we could. To senior
staffers, the solution was simple; we built more training facili-
ties closer to our home base so we could be home with our families at night or during the day if we were not training. But as
the Training Officer, I knew it was more complicated than it
looked. When you travel, you can fully immerse yourself in the
training; your focus is on the job rather than on your kid's soccer game or mowing the lawn. When you're on the road but
not training, you are still immersed in the job, maintaining your
gear and studying tactics and other critical pieces of warfare,
as well as bonding and building teamwork. In addition, going
home and losing focus makes training more dangerous and
causes more accidents, just like in combat. When you are close
to redeploying, your focus can quickly shift to thinking about
home—which can be lethal.

Although distractions aren't necessarily life-threatening at
work, they do interfere with performance. It's a good idea for
teams to get away from their workspaces when collaborating

on critical group projects or even periodically; the immersion forces people to focus. Off-site meetings are great, but unless we set the conditions by taking away phones and ensuring team members stop answering emails on their computers during the working groups, we won't get the excellence that we are looking for.

Try to work out a plan, solve a problem, or develop a concept in two different environments: one, a "high interrupt" space, such as a regular office, and another, in which you have carefully insulated the environment from outside distractions. Observe which environment is better for focus and more conducive to producing better work. Do you save time? Come to better conclusions? Get everyone on board faster? How much does the deliberately crafted environment help your focus?

> **Your best results occur when you're "all-in" and distractions are minimized.**

Meditation and Maintaining Focus

How many of us have picked up a book and read a page or two, only to realize you don't remember what you just read, and now you have to reread those pages. (Of course that would *not* happen with this book!) Focus is a muscle, and like any muscle, it can be taught and trained. For years, I was fascinated with the Eastern practice of Zen and meditation while conducting foreign internal defense in Southeast Asia.

> **Focus is a muscle; it can be
> taught and trained.**

Thailand was one of my favorite countries to work in. I spent a lot of time there working with the Thai SEALs and loved it. It was there that I began practicing meditation and mindfulness more than two decades ago, quickly realizing that it was very powerful for training my focus, thus making me a better and more productive SEAL.

Eventually, the SEAL Teams realized the power of meditation, and have implemented it into the training. I'm happy to say that I was able to assist in that process of making it part of the resiliency program. Meditation is a significant focus workout for any SEAL operator. Of course, in the beginning, we had to fight ingrained beliefs many of us had about meditation; it isn't typically found in a conventional military playbook. But many aspects of meditation, including the spiritual ones, help us get into and stay in the right frame of mind as an operator, a warrior, and even a Blue-Collar Scholar. It has worked with SEALs, and if it works for SEALs, then I know it can work for you, too.

A 2015 *Washington Post* article described a scientist seeing the benefits of meditation and mindfulness in brain scans. Just eight weeks of meditation increased the volume of the brain in five regions: the areas that control the wandering mind, learning, memory, emotional regulation, empathy and compassion, and neurotransmitter production.

Focus on the Present

If you can't focus on the present, you are focusing on something that isn't there yet (the future) or something you won't have again (the past). We must be aware and play offense with our focus. We must train ourselves to control it, and not just let it run wild on its own.

When distracted, I use the mantra "focus, focus, focus" until I regain the mindfulness of being in the present and immersed in what I am doing. In war, people often develop anxiety even when they are not engaged in combat and have to be sent home. They worry about a random rocket or mortar attack, awfulize, and focus on those future threats, instead of the moment they are in.

The Japanese have a beautiful concept called Ichigyo Zammai, which means "full concentration on a single act." People who practice this make their lives a piece of art by focusing on a single action at any given time. We all fall in the trap of doing something while we believe we should be doing something else. We live in the future and become frustrated in the present; we don't actually experience what we are living and doing.

> **Focus on the future, and you'll focus on something that doesn't yet exist.**
>
> **Focus on the past, and you'll focus on something you won't have again.**
>
> **Stay focused on the present.**

Shifting Focus Away from Pain

We make our expectations to students clear: the only easy day was yesterday. You'll feel discomfort for your whole career; it's part of the job description. They know they'll have to be at their best in the worst of times, when they're cold, wet, scared, and exhausted. So we immediately teach them how to focus when they are in pain and discomfort. Often, we will put them in the pushup position, like the plank, and leave them there for an hour or so, sometimes while teaching classes. When they start to fidget and begin moaning and sighing, we tell them to shut up and stop hurting everyone around them with their suffering. Isopraxism is the mirroring effect, meaning people around you mirror your behavior. If a teammate allows himself to suffer, it's like a disease; it will spread quickly. I say "allows himself to suffer" because suffering is a choice—and we can control our choices.

At this point, I explain to students how they can use a first strike approach to *shift their focus*. I say: "Make an adjustment. Put more weight on your left hand, arch your back just a little, and keep adjusting to shift the discomfort. Make a mental game of it, and use as many body parts as you can." When they do, they learn to control what they focus on and learn to distance themselves from pain. If they continue to focus their minds on the pain, it reinforces the idea of the pain, and this establishes a terrible relationship with discomfort. But if they focus their full attention on taking the offensive, and taking action, no matter how small, they are able to distance themselves from the pain.

> **Take the offensive, control what you focus on, and distance yourself from pain.**

The goal for the students is to wear out their bodies equally, to make every body part carry the load, not just the arms and back. Shifting their weight and shifting their focus means their concentration on pain doesn't build up. It's a handy tool in all aspects of life, not just the physical. By sharing the load among body parts, you can focus on the parts, not the pain. The pain will become more distant, but you must be offensive and take the first strike. Your body is an organism—a team—so share the load. Make adjustments in life, shift your focus, and change your experience and results.

Early in the Vietnam War, in 1963, Vietnamese Buddhist monk Thich Quang Duc protested against his government for religious equality and freedom. Duc sat lotus style on a Saigon street while two other monks doused him with gasoline and then set him afire. Duc never moved from his position; he stayed wholly focused in meditation. Malcolm Browne captured the event and was awarded a Pulitzer Prize for his photograph of this seemingly serene monk sitting in the street in flames, unmoving. Duc had spent most of his life learning to control his focus by meditating for long periods. By doing so, he had created distance between himself and the pain that we can only imagine. This may be an extreme example of focusing, but it illustrates its tremendous power and what it can enable us to withstand.

> In combat focus, every sense is magnified,
> and everything happening around you makes
> sense before your conscious mind can
> "talk about it."

Moving Meditation

In the late 1990s, an Apache trained me and a platoon mate to become expert trackers. We lived in the woods, ate off the land, did sweat lodges, and studied tracking all day, with our faces in the dirt. One of the native techniques we learned seemed a little odd to me at first. It was called the "fox walk." We received detailed instructions on how to walk like a fox in the grass, with our shoes off so that we could feel the earth (50 percent of our nerve endings are in our face, hands, and feet). If you ever watch a fox walk, there are no wasted movements; it walks with extreme purpose. The fox walks using a "direct register," meaning it places its back feet perfectly within its front tracks, leaving only two noticeable tracks in the dirt, appearing to be a two-legged animal. Walking with a direct register also makes minimal noise; the fox isn't disturbing new ground. An interesting fact: a feral cat does the same thing but a house cat doesn't. The house cat doesn't hunt to live so it can afford to be sloppy and noisy.

The fox walk was intended to get us into "the spirit world" and become aware of nature. It makes you focus on the small details so that you walk with extremely deliberate intent. If you lose focus, you get sloppy and awkward, so you have to refocus on the performance points of the walk. This technique is an offensive reverse evolution technique: you walk like you are stalking. When you focus on the details, your state of mind changes. Your self-talk stops, the worry of the world ends, and your senses wake up; this is where the "spirit world" is—it's in the present moment. You then begin to feel what's around you, and your subconscious mind opens up to new information and intuition.

I call this practice *moving mediation*. It's reversing the alpha state by focusing your mind on the details of the walk, moving your body deliberately, and creating a rhythm that can be repeated—just like Marines do when they march. Marines spend numerous hours perfecting a march, fingers aligned, stomach in, head level, eyes forward, foot striking the ground with exactness. Being deliberate and intentional draws your focus into the present.

EXERCISE

When you are present, your senses are heightened, and your intuition comes forward—you feel your environment. In your mind's eye, focus on seeing radar rings pulsing from your head and traveling from close to far, taking your eyes and ears with them. Your listening focus goes from close to 10 feet, then 20 feet, and so on. Just like if you are at a party and hear something 10 feet away that catches your ear, you can laser focus on it and ignore someone talking close by; you can control your listening focus. You don't have to be moving to practice focusing. You can be still, but the key is to control your attention and not to focus on yourself.

> **The key to laser focus is not to focus on yourself.**

You will notice things that you have never seen. Sitting in a restaurant or a park bench or your office, focus on the rings and what is around you.

When you laser focus, that blabbermouth in your mind stops talking. Neuroscience calls this the default mode network (DMN), the "me" part of the brain that focuses on the future and the past, not the present. Meditators and others who can focus can slow down this area of the brain willfully. This is where your situational awareness (the spirit world) lies.

Now imagine that you are having a conversation with a colleague. Instead of thinking about how you are going to respond to her, you listen actively and intentionally, with focus. The result is an active and authentic conversation that produces results and doesn't allow the ego to take over.

TAKEAWAYS

- The direction you focus on is the direction you will follow.

- Don't look where you don't want to go.

- Discipline is focus; focus is discipline.

- Focus turns us from transactional to transformational individuals.

- Total focus requires total immersion and commitment. Your best results are achieved when you remove as many distractions as possible.

- Meditation helps you calm down, empathize, and focus.

- Take the offensive. Focus on what's in front of you, what's in the present, and distance yourself from pain.

- Moving meditation—meditating while otherwise occupied—keeps you focused and moving forward while also heightening your sensitivity to your surroundings.

- Extreme focus allows you to notice what you wouldn't have noticed otherwise. It enables active listening, which results in more connected authentic conversations.

[handwritten note: analogy m to f muzzle faus]

5

FIRST STRIKE MINDSET

Developing Language Discipline

In a remote area in North Queensland, Australia, an aboriginal tribe offers some insight into how critical language can be and how it shapes how we see the world and life in general. The Guugu Yimithirr tribe has a unique, almost magical ability to orient themselves and successfully navigate the world around them, no matter where they may be. They seem to have an invisible compass that enables them to feel Earth's magnetic fields.

What's the secret behind this tribe's ability to know their location and direction at all times? The answer is simple: language. The language most of us use employs *egocentric* directions, which describe the relationship of an object or place relative to one's self. We are at the center, and we use such words as *left*, *right*, *front*, and *back* relative to ourselves. The Guugu

Yimithirr tribe, on the other hand, uses *cardinal* directions or *geographic* directions: north, south, east, and west.

They don't have words that place them at the center of the directions they are giving. They wouldn't say: "To the right of the parking lot, there is a building. Go in the first door, take the third hallway to your left, continue until the end, and then take a right down another hallway." Instead, they would say, "Go to the building north of the parking lot. Go in the first door, and then go west at the third hallway. Continue to the end and go north down another hallway." If they were line dancers, their directions might go something like: "Face to the north, two steps to the east, two steps to the west. Now spin to the east, now spin to the west, etc."

The Guugu Yimithirr don't have words for "left," "right," "front," and "back." They teach their children at the age of seven geographical orientation. By shaping their language this way, the children grow up paying attention to their physical environment and the clues it gives. They feel where the sun, moon, and wind are, and can find most anything as it relates to these.

Language has the power to shape our minds and to shape outcomes. It's a filter of perception, memory, and attention, so it can ultimately be used as a tool for or against us. How we use it is our choice.

BE THE CAUSE, NOT THE EFFECT

"First strike" and "first strike mindset" are maxims from the SEAL playbook that convey the seizing of the initiative and taking the advantage by acting or moving first. You make the enemy respond to your moves, rather than letting them take the initiative, forcing you to respond to them. The fundamental concept of the first strike is a form of inverse evolution: "being the cause of the effect, not the effect that was caused."

According to the belief in evolution, it is not the strongest of the species that survives, nor the most intelligent. It is the one most adaptable to change. My goal is to help you understand how to shape your world to evolve, not by chance, but by design, and to do that through language.

> **Fight like you picked it;**
> **live your life like you chose it.**

Language Is a Weapon to Take the Initiative: Use It

By controlling your language, both internal and external, you start to form a different relationship with life and your place in it. You can even change your beliefs by having the discipline to control what language you use. It's not tough to do. You just need to be conscious of it, and have faith that what you are doing will transform you.

Remember, if we embrace accountability and extreme ownership of our lives, we love them more. It means we own the future, and everything in our past that got us to this point. The victim mindset is the opposite. Victims point fingers and make excuses for their present state, meaning that their dubious past owns their future. This fuels anger, fear, negativity, and an overwhelming sense of being out of control. The feeling of loss of control can lead to depression and apathy.

> **Language is a compass that can guide you in the direction you wish to travel.**

Avoiding "Maybe"

As Yoda famously said in *The Empire Strikes Back,* "Do or do not. There is no try." When you add the word *maybe* to anything, you might as well admit you won't do it. *Maybe* is a powerful failure word.

The online invitation company Evite will only let you take "Maybe" off as a response if you pay for premium service. You either commit or you don't. That is why you have to pay to get that button removed—commitment has value.

> **In the invitation world as in ours, you either commit or you don't.**

When I made changes in my life, I had to accept where I was and control my thoughts through my language. I had to quit awfulizing. Once you start awfulizing, it gains speed and momentum. There was no "maybe." I either did it or didn't, and it was my choice because I was accountable for my life and well-being. Just like any order that I have ever given, I didn't give myself wiggle room. I told myself, "Listen up! This is what you're doing!"

Here's the rule of thumb: when you are giving an order, there are no maybes. Don't even hedge with "I've decided." The way to give an order is to state it: "This is what we are doing!" This takes the possibility of another option off the table, and makes it clear the discussion is over.

> **Life is like a mirror. It reflects back what you think and believe.**

LANGUAGE AS PART OF ORGANIZATIONAL CULTURE

As SEALs, we have cultural words and expressions that shape us into the force that we are. Every person and every team— SEALs or otherwise—should have a cultural language that is guarded fervently. While patrolling on a mission, depending on the terrain, SEALs may take a break every hour to rest and regroup. When we stop, we don't just flop down on the ground, we form a predetermined perimeter around the terrain, as close to a circle as we can. Firepower is spread out evenly around the perimeter, so we have balanced protection and are ready to fight in any direction. The perimeter is sacred. Anything inside is good; anything outside is a potential threat. Our language should be treated like our perimeters. We should protect it and not allow defeatism, complaining, awfulizing, and general negativity to penetrate it.

> Language is part of an organization's culture; it defines the perimeter that protects the organization and its ethos.

In BUD/S training, we must brief our doctors and medical staff on the concept of organizational language and culture. Countless times, I've seen a student go to medical and never come back. When a student gets there, the staff often—consciously or subconsciously—feels sorry for the student. Before you know it, the student feels sorry for himself and quits. In BUD/S, medical is known as the expressway to quitting, and most students avoid it like the plague. Students need to go to medical if they are hurt, so we now place SEAL instructors in the medical room to ensure doctors respect our organizational culture. It's a hard balance to manage.

Wrong Focus Leads to Failure

The human mind is designed to see danger and focus on it, so we tend to dwell on it if we don't intentionally control our thoughts. I never let the sounds of fear and doubt come out of my mouth, and I sure as hell didn't want them to go into my ears and into my mind. When I was leading missions in some of the most dangerous places in the world, I sat the intelligence officers down and gave them explicit orders not to mention improvised explosive devices (IEDs) more than once during their intelligence brief. In some cities, IEDs were so prevalent, it was almost certain you would encounter them. Nobody likes the thought of seeing a big white flash and possibly being instantly killed or maimed. Fear and doubt are contagious and will spread like wildfire.

When I train people in these concepts, their fears immediately come to the surface. They will say things like, "You don't understand, (fill in the blank) happened to me," or "You don't always win; sometimes you fail." My response is always, "Of course there are times you will fail, but focusing on it will make it more likely."

> **If you control your language,
> you control your life.**

THE LANGUAGE OF GRATITUDE

When I look back on my life, I do so with gratitude and give thanks for my success. I'm grateful for the tough environment I grew up in because it strengthened me and enabled me to be a SEAL. I'm grateful to have been poor and gone through hard times because impoverished people who suffer tend to develop a strong sense of empathy for others. I got to serve and fight in three different wars. Had I not, I don't believe I would have developed the deep love and gratitude that I have for this country and what it affords me. I know this country isn't perfect, but I have chosen to focus on what it *does* provide me, not what it *doesn't*. When you travel around the world and live in countries with extreme poverty and suffering, it brings perspective and engenders a strong sense of gratitude. I am thankful for everything—even a difficult past—that has led to my success. Most people don't credit their challenging backgrounds for their success, but it's a beneficial concept to keep in mind and practice. If you can love who you are, then everything that happened to you contributed to you being you.

Reframing: Focusing on the Glass Half Full

One powerful communication tactic I've used to elicit positive focus is *reframing*. When I see a student shaking violently from being wet and cold, I would often say to him: "You're lucky you get to stand up here, shaking with some of the hardest men on Earth. What a gift!" I would always see the confusion in his eyes, but eventually, he understood. We empathize but we don't sympathize, as we want to avoid training students to feel sorry for themselves. The sympathy mindset will clearly hinder their ability to accomplish the mission.

At work, if you think, "I have to present to the CEO and her staff," reframe that to "I *get* to present to the CEO and her staff." In your personal life, if you think, "I have to go to the gym," shift your language to " I *get* to go to the gym." Take whatever dread

"I have TO" → "I get to"

you have, shift into gratitude mode, and finish sentences and thoughts with gratitude. I remember when the 9/11 terrorist attacks happened, and I wasn't part of the first wave of deployments to Afghanistan, my family said, "Thank God, you don't have to go." My response was, "I don't *get* to go." A few words can shift everything. Over time, they will change your performance and ultimately your outlook on life.

NO PITY ALLOWED

In 2007, while conducting a mission in Fallujah, Iraq, Navy SEAL Lieutenant Jason Redman came under heavy fire during a direct action mission. He and his two teammates were wounded. Jason was shot twice in the arm and once directly in the face. His helmet, night vision goggles, and body armor were also shot up. This gunfight was at point-blank range in thick weeds, so it was a very lethal and violent confrontation. Just like the Chief, he and his team didn't quit; they won the fight. But that's not what made Jason a legend, it's what he did next that did.

A few weeks later, as he was recovering from his life-threatening wounds, Jason did something that still inspires people around the world. He managed to write a letter that he had the staff post on the front door of his hospital room in Bethesda Naval Hospital in Maryland. The letter read:

> ATTENTION—To all those who enter here. If you are coming into this room with sorrow or to feel sorry for

my wounds, go elsewhere. The wounds I received I got in a job I love, doing it for people I love, supporting the freedom of a country I deeply love. I am incredibly tough and will make a full recovery. What is full? That is the absolute utmost physically my body has the ability to recover. Then I will push that about 20 percent further through sheer mental tenacity. This room you are about to enter is a room of fun, optimism, and intense rapid regrowth. If you are not prepared for that, go elsewhere.

The management.

Jason understood that he needed to write that letter and to go on the offensive with his recovery. Alphas don't allow feeling sorry for themselves because they are not victims. Jason knew that he had to design his environment. He understood accountability, so he focused on the future, not the past. He controlled the language around him to help with his recovery. He may not necessarily have felt that way at first, but he shaped the conversation in his environment, so that he could control how he would evolve. Jason came to this point and said to himself: "F*** it. It's time to move on." The emotional power of saying "f*** it" helped Jason make a decision and move on, not looking backward or dragging a victim mentality forward. Once Jason made that decision, he could move on, but not before. It was his choice, and he made it.

Jason knew that people would naturally feel sorry for him. When he committed and put that note on the door, it also gave him the external motivation to live up to what he had declared. He knew what he was doing; he had manufactured his own motivation.

> **Give empathy, not sympathy, because sympathy makes people feel sorry for themselves.**

DEVELOPING THE CAN-DO MINDSET

One of the primary traits we cultivate in SEALs is problem solving. We create a problem-solving mindset by changing our language, so it doesn't allow people to quit on a problem. SEALs learn that quitting is not an option. In our ethos, we declare, "I will never quit," "I am never out of the fight," and "I will not fail." This is part of our daily language and becomes part of how we judge each other in the team.

Our nation expects us to solve problems under extreme duress and in challenging circumstances. When we don't know, we find out. When discussing an ambiguous situation and I don't know the answer, I *say* that I will find out. Finishing a sentence or a discussion with that phrase creates an evolutionary, problem-solving way of thinking.

You may not feel that way in your work or personal lives as you read this, and I say not *yet*! Practice! Practice makes permanent, and perfect practice makes perfect permanence. To develop a can-do attitude, practicing internal and external language control will help create a default first strike mindset.

> **Practicing internal and external language control will help create a default first strike mind.**

The Value of "Not Yet"

Controlling the language you use to talk to yourself and to talk to others will shape who you are and how you react to the world—and it can do the same for others. This is why when students are in discomfort, we don't allow them to complain or to make sounds of weakness. We don't want them to infect the other students around them. Defeatist language will cause fear and doubt and undermine motivation, shaping your beliefs in yourself and those around you.

We often give students tasks outside their skill sets and knowledge. When we ask them if they know something or can do something, the only acceptable responses are "Yes" or "Not yet, but I will find out." "Yet" is the evolutionary term because we train ourselves to understand that we will eventually figure it out. This simple concept ingrains the belief that nothing is out of reach.

Phrases like "I'm not good at (fill in the blank)," "I don't understand (fill in the blank)," "This isn't working," and so on, spell trouble. When you allow yourself to end a dialogue on those thoughts, you stop improving in areas that mean something to you. You need to complete the sentence or thought with "yet" or "I will figure it out." Challenge yourself never to finish with a negative thought. End your statements positively, and for goodness sake, stop defeatism. When you catch yourself awfulizing, you must redirect your language even if you don't feel it . . . *yet*! Every sentence, every word, and every thought gives your mind proof of positive outcomes, and the more proof you have, the more likely you are to change your mind and beliefs.

> **When you catch yourself awfulizing, you must redirect your language even if you don't feel it . . . *yet*.**

FIRST STRIKE LANGUAGE

The first strike methodology calls for being on the offensive, setting high expectations, and falling in love with adversity. The Pygmalion effect is a phenomenon in which other people's expectations affect the target person's performance, while the Galatea effect refers to how our personal expectations of ourselves affect our own performance. Performance is largely self-driven but can be heavily influenced by others. In any case, achievement starts with disciplined, offensive-minded first strike language.

> Achievement starts with disciplined,
> offensive-minded first strike language.

The Only Easy Day Was Yesterday

Above the entrance to our training facility there is an old wooden sign that reads: "The only easy day was yesterday." It means that when you enter this world, you expect adversity. We also say: "If it doesn't suck, we don't do it." Both these phrases clearly set the expectations of what Navy SEAL life will be like.

I often hear people say that SEALs love pain. That's not it. Ultimately, we have learned to form a different relationship with discomfort because we volunteered for this life and that is our choice.

You use first strike language to create an environment that changes you. You don't allow the environment to determine your language (i.e., "This sucks. We shouldn't have to do this."). I call this "first strike inverse evolution." When you change your language about discomfort or pain, you change how you feel about both.

We don't allow students to complain, whine, moan, sigh, pout, or yell during physical training events because feeling sorry for themselves is a clear path to failure. It reinforces in their minds that straining and discomfort are terrible, and they begin to focus on the pain and forge a lousy relationship with it. We teach them instead to embrace it. We explain to them that civilians describe what they are feeling as pain, but we like to refer to it as weakness leaving the body. This sparks them to yell out "HOOYAH" or "Yeeeaaaaa!" This, in turn, starts to anchor their belief that, as German philosopher Friedrich Nietzsche said, "That which does not kill me, makes me stronger."[1]

While uncontrolled language *represents* your thoughts and feelings, controlled language can *shape* your thoughts and feelings.

I remember going through my own training as a student. At this point, there were fewer than 20 of us from a class that started with roughly 150 students. We were standing on a berm, freezing. It may sound sadistic, but my instructor spoke in a very nonchalant, matter-of-fact way, not as if he was talking to someone who was freezing to death, but like he was having a coaching session with me. "Hiner, I want you to look around. I want you to imagine how many people out there wish they had the GUTS to stand on this f***ing berm, jackhammering in the middle of the night with the rest of these crazy motherf***ers. But you know what, they don't have the GUTS that you do. You are one hard motherf***er. Now hit the f***ing surf and get wet and sandy." Even though hitting the freezing surf and being wet is always the hardest part of the training, my response was loud and proud, "HOOYAH!" I got goosebumps that night, and my association with discomfort was changed forever. It was an emotionally charged moment that I return to in times of adversity. Every time I think about it, I get goosebumps.

Our relationship with straining, discomfort, and fear need to be nurtured. When we change our language around an event, we start to change our relationship with that event. I remember one night during Hell Week—it was Wednesday, the fourth night without any sleep. I was standing on top of a berm, soaking wet, having just gotten out of the 55-degree water of the Pacific Ocean, with a 45-degree breeze blowing hard off the water. As I stood there, shaking so hard it looked like I was having a seizure, one of the instructors walked up to me and started a conversation as if we were at a family gathering. He didn't at all acknowledge my discomfort. It dawned on me that it wasn't because he didn't care. He cared intensely; that is why he didn't feel sorry for me. He knew I was evolving.

EXERCISE

Pay attention to what you say and how you say it. Write down what your default defensive language is. When you hear yourself using defensive language, immediately correct yourself and reframe your language and thoughts toward the desired outcome. Go on the offense. This an important way to train your mind, which I will discuss in detail in a later chapter.

TAKEAWAYS

- Language has the power to shape our minds and our outcomes.

- According to Charles Darwin, "It is not the strongest of the species that survives, nor the most intelligent that survives. It is the one that is most adaptable to change."

- "Be the cause, not the effect" is a central SEAL maxim that applies to communication as well as to action.

- Language is a powerful tool. By controlling your language, you can take the initiative, change your belief and that of others, and define your role in your organization and in your life. Language becomes a vital part of the first strike mindset.

- Organizational language and culture are important. A negative mentality will spread like wildfire and lead to failure.

- Never complete a negative thought. Reframe it to match your desired outcome.

- Disciplined first strike language and the language of gratitude lead to positive focus and achievement.

- Use empathy, not sympathy. Sympathy makes people feel sorry for themselves, clearing a path to failure.

- When everyone in a work environment has a first strike, can-do attitude, this positive mindset becomes contagious, creates its own momentum, and accomplishes great things.

6

THE HABIT OF WINNING

When Second Place
Isn't Good Enough

On the beaches of Coronado during BUD/S training you can hear the instructors yelling from afar: "It pays to be a winner, gents!" When the students hear those words, they know what is coming. They will be divided into six-man boat crews and will compete in a race or an "evolution," a sequence of races and other activities. We put students of the same height in boat crews to equalize the load in each boat. Winners and winners only are rewarded because in our business, second place in a gunfight doesn't earn you a trophy; it puts you in a box to be carried home. There is no second place—a concept fundamental to elite organizations—and to anyone aspiring to be the best they can be.

We line up the boat crews on the beach for a briefing. Each team carries a 200-pound rubber boat on their heads, which, as you can imagine, is not exactly pleasant. The boat is merely a tool we use to make the students uncomfortable and to force teamwork. The event may go something like this: each crew will conduct races 500 meters down the beach, and the winner of each race gets to sit down by their boats. The other teams line up again and race, and that winner gets to sit down and rest, and so on until only one team remains. That losing team "gets" to hit the surf; there is nothing a student likes less than getting wet and sandy. The students understand that the winners are rewarded with rest, while the losers do the entire evolution, including getting wet and sandy. The motivation to *not* finish second is high, which creates tremendous focus.

NEVER PRACTICE LOSING

It is human nature to focus on faults and failures. Most organizations focus on what isn't working and what people are *doing* wrong. But good leaders and self-leaders focus on what is going right and reward that behavior because that feedback reinforces winning and creates good organizational habits. Successful, well-recognized teams develop and maintain good practices and serve as models for others, while poorly performing teams don't know what success looks like and even successful teams that go unrewarded may fail to sustain good practices permanently. That doesn't mean leaders should focus only on the good stuff— it's important to correct mistakes—but an emphasis on positive actions can deliver better results faster because most people don't have a problem seeing the errors.

> **Don't find faults; doing that creates a losing mentality.**
>
> **Focus on what you and your team are doing right.**

By the way, which crew do you think wins most of the races? It's usually the boat crew with the shortest students (we call them "Smurfs"). We've never done a scientific study on why Smurfs tend to win. From my experience, they win because they focus on teamwork and strategy, knowing that their stride is shorter and they are carrying a higher percentage of their body weight on their heads. Because they are at a physical disadvantage, they have to work smarter.

> **Focus on teamwork and strategy, rather than relying on raw talent alone.**

In our training, we never play dead, and we never stop fighting even when it appears we have been shot or "killed" in a scenario. We never quit; we continue fighting until we win—just like the Chief in Chapter 2 did. *We never practice losing.* Yes, this seems obvious, but people continually practice losing with their focus and internal self-deprecation. In our work and lives, if we use defensive language or succumb to awfulizing, we are, in a sense, practicing to lose. Remember, what comes out of our mouths is an indication of what goes on in our minds.

> **Never practice losing—you'll end up getting a lot of practice.**

MANUFACTURING MOTIVATION: ONE DOSE AT A TIME

Winning is an addiction, and losing is a disease. Let's pause for a moment to put some blue-collar science behind that statement.

In our bodies we have more than 100 neurotransmitters, chemical messengers that transmit information to our nerves, muscles, and glands. They are used by the brain to help regulate digestion, breathing, and heartbeat. They affect focus, sleep, and mood, and they drive our behaviors. For my purposes, I'll discuss four key neurotransmitters: dopamine, oxytocin, serotonin, and endorphins—a grouping I will refer to as "DOSE."

Dopamine: The Reward of Pleasure

Among its many functions, dopamine motivates us to achieve, to act to fulfill our desired goals. It's a habit-forming, addictive neurotransmitter that gives us pleasure when released. Drugs such as cocaine, opiates, amphetamines, nicotine, and alcohol all increase levels of dopamine, which in turn signals our reward system. Behaviors like gambling, sex, and eating are driven by rewards of dopamine.

To create positive habits, we must understand dopamine and take the first-strike approach to produce it. Praise, accolades, compliments, and other reinforcing language trigger a release of dopamine in our bodies. But the odd thing about good habits is that the reward often comes later, not at the time of the action. The reward for eating well takes time; we don't lose weight overnight. In weightlifting, it takes time for the muscles to respond and grow. The reward for bad habits, on the other hand, is instant gratification: As soon as someone uses drugs or eats a slice of cake, he is high on dopamine. When a gambler walks into a casino and hears the slot machines ringing—"ding, ding, ding, ding, ding!"—and the coins falling, she gets a shot of dopamine, and those shots keep coming until she's penniless. This is why bad habits are easily formed.

> **Discipline is all about delaying gratification.**

The key to delaying gratification is to focus on the moment and win it! During Hell Week, the alternative is to succumb to the pleasure of stopping to rest, wrapping yourself in a blanket, and taking the boat off your head. The trouble is, once you stop, it's hard to get back into the moment, and when you do, it seems harder than it was before. Getting into the moment and staying there will get you through adversity more quickly and with less pain. And when you finally get the reward, the pain will be long past.

Self-Leadership and the Importance of Rewards

Good habits take time and more than just willpower; they take offensive action. By recognizing success in ourselves and in our teams, we get a quick dose of dopamine. We need to celebrate good, positive behaviors along the way, rewarding everything we are doing right. *Ding, ding, ding, ding!* These small celebrations create habits and a "habitude" (habits of attitude) as these recognized successes create proof for our belief in ourselves and our teams.

Think about the power of social media and how it shapes our beliefs and actions. Those who follow you control your actions by clicking the "like" button. Every like is a little dose rewarding your behavior, so the more likes you get, the more you post similar content. In your work and home life, find the "like" buttons and don't be afraid to push them to celebrate victories. If you are a leader, lead with likes. Identify and praise what people are doing well. By the same token, like yourself—recognize when you do something good as well.

> **Lead others—and yourself—with "likes."**

When I formed my writing habit, which I definitely had fears and doubts about, I rewarded myself for getting out of the bed at 4:30 a.m. and getting my fingers on the computer keyboard with a delicious cup of bulletproof coffee, coffee that has a little MCT oil (a brain function-enhancing nutrition supplement) and butter. Delicious! I created a new relationship with my writing, and what I once dreaded has become fun and enjoyable. Now when I wake up, I'm excited and don't have issues getting in front of the computer.

When I mine a nugget of "thought gold" from my mind, I celebrate and congratulate myself; sometimes I do a little dance in my office. There are so many good ways to create dopamine: exercise, music, and meditation, among others. We can use these to help create the habits we want and gain the success we desire. We can manufacture motivation; we just need to go on the offensive.

> **We can manufacture motivation;**
> **we just need to go on the offensive.**

Oxytocin: The Love Drug

Sometimes called the "love drug," oxytocin forges relationships and builds trust and intimacy. During pregnancy and birth, a woman's oxytocin levels skyrocket, which is nature's way of bonding mother and child. The simple act of touching someone—respectfully and appropriately, of course!—can help build connection and strengthen your influence as a leader. Even a single hand on a shoulder when complimenting or praising a team member can go a long way.

Humans are designed to work in teams and to sacrifice for one another. This helps ensure our survival; we need each other. However, when Covid-19 swept the country, and the sacrifice asked of us forced us to stay apart from each other and to avoid group gatherings, we saw how isolation and disconnectedness impacted the mental health and well-being of our society. It's unnatural for us to be apart for extended periods of time.

There is a special bond between SEALs who went through BUD/S, especially Hell Week, together that remains for life. During training, you are always cold and wet, so every chance you get, you huddle together for warmth. Even when standing in line, you lean so close into the person in front of you that no space exists between you. If the instructors wish to punish the class, all they need to do is say: "Spread out." They know how important it is to maintain body contact in order to warm up. This amount of contact during training contributes to the bonds we form for life.

Serotonin: The Happy Chemical

Commonly referred to as the ultimate happy chemical, serotonin makes you feel significant and important, boosting confidence and helping you succeed. Gratitude increases serotonin levels and makes you happier. Serotonin also either directly or indirectly influences many of the functions that are key to our success and well-being, such as sleep, memory, appetite, and even sexual desire.

Most of the medication prescribed to treat depression and anxiety consists of selective serotonin reuptake inhibitors (SSRIs), which block the reabsorption of serotonin, therefore making more serotonin available. Seasonal affective disorder (SAD) is caused when diminished sunlight triggers a drop in serotonin levels, resulting in depression. I experienced this when I spent nearly six weeks in Norway during the winter. The sun never came up. It was dark the entire time, and it definitely affected me. Although I loved Norway, all I wanted to do was hit a beach and get some rays.

Endorphins: The Body's Painkiller

Endorphins are produced by our nervous system to help us deal with pain and stress. They are the body's painkiller and make us feel good. Have you heard of the "runner's high"? It's the euphoric feeling caused by the release of endorphins that follows a run, workout, or other exercise. Listening to music, laughing, having sex, and eating chocolate also trigger the release of endorphins. When we are high on endorphins, the executive part of our brains wakes up, and our ability to think and solve problems improves. We become more productive.

Cortisol: A Losing Path

When I said winning is an addiction and losing is a disease, I meant it literally. Why is losing a disease? Because fear, shame, anxiety, and stress trigger the production of cortisol, which is our body's built-in alarm system. It fuels our fight-or-flight instinct, and helps us survive, but if too much accumulates over time, it can kill you. It's beneficial to us when we are in danger, but having it present all the time is harmful.

Someone who is working in a toxic environment, being judged or insulted constantly, also experiences a constant drip of cortisol. It's like an IV dripping sickness, apathy, and a lack of productivity into their veins. The more we stress, the less we can think. Our performance on complicated tasks decreases, which in turn increases our fears, so we produce more cortisol, and the cycle continues.

Cortisol does strange things not only to our minds, but also to our bodies. We heal more slowly and bruise more easily, and our skin gets thinner. It may even cause acne. Here's an interesting fact: soldiers in Iraq, on average, gained 10 pounds on deployment. Why? Cortisol makes you crave sweets to build a store of quick energy for fight or flight. I know, it's counterintuitive. You'd think all the stress and hard work in combat would cause you to lose weight, but, no, you actually may gain it!

Stress and Body Chemistry

After my last deployment to Afghanistan, I went to see one of the doctors who worked with the SEAL Teams. He drew blood samples from older SEALs with multiple combat tours under their belts to see the effects of combat and stress on our body chemistry. The results were not surprising: high levels of cortisol. At the time, I was in great shape from regular training, but the negative compounding effects of elevated levels of cortisol had wreaked havoc on my mood, productivity, sleep, and overall wellness. Beyond that, I had the testosterone level of a person 30 years older, even though I was training heavily with weights. Constant stress is a disease; it will infiltrate all parts of your life, zapping productivity. It will kill you if you don't treat it.

Managing Your DOSE

As mentioned, for simplicity, I use the acronym DOSE to refer to the neurotransmitters dopamine, oxytocin, serotonin, and endorphins. I will also use DOSE when I describe ways to form habits and get in a better state of mind.

Language matters: a single word can trigger different neurotransmitters, and give us either a DOSE or a disease. Over time, the language we *choose* will have consequences not only on our performance but also on our health and relationships. When we *choose* to focus, we can influence the timing and rate at which these neurotransmitters are produced. Discipline is about delaying gratification. If we can focus on the moment and delay gratification, we can win the moment. With each moment, we gain momentum with small victories, each time giving ourselves a DOSE. Each DOSE fuels more positive moments, so stay focused!

> **A single word can give us a DOSE,**
>
> **or it can give us a disease.**

These seemingly small adjustments over time remind me of compounding interest and the rule of 72. The rule is simple: if you receive compounded interest in an investment, you can divide 72 by your return percentage to find out how many years it will take you to double your money. For instance: if your return is 12 percent a year, you double your money in six years. Like compounded interest, small wins executed steadily over time grow into something more significant. GUTS is like getting a little return on every part of your life. Imagine, if you build motivation, discipline, and good habits at a rate of 2 percent each week—in 36 weeks, you will be twice as good as you were when you started!

> **Much like financial compounding, the compound effects of steady drips of positivity can add up quickly. So, too, can drips of negativity take you in the other direction.**

Every action is a vote. To win the election, you don't have to be perfect; you just need to win the most votes. It's easy for us to fall into the all-or-nothing mode, but it's more important to keep making incremental progress.

FEEDBACK LOOP: THE AFTER ACTION REVIEW

In a dangerous profession, lessons are often "written in blood," meaning mistakes may cost someone his or her life or limb. In business, mistakes may not be a matter of life and death, but they can still be costly. However, mistakes aren't all bad. They are also opportunities to learn and evolve; in that way, they can be treasures.

When something goes wrong, SEALs spend an enormous amount of time and energy dissecting the evolution to identify the reasons the mistake was made to ensure it never happens again. We also acknowledge what we did right to enforce that behavior and to anchor good habits and habitudes of continuous improvement. We never waste an opportunity to learn. This process of recall, learning, and evolving is called an After Action Review, or AAR.

The process is quite simple. It mostly consists of awareness and acceptance; over time, the process becomes a habit, a routine part of life. An organization must have what we call an *economy of motion*, so that all learning leads to prioritization and streamlining for greater productivity. We keep what is useful and discard what is not. For example, in combat shooting, our goal is to put a bullet as quickly and accurately exactly where we want it. Every movement that doesn't facilitate this we discard. There are no wasted movements.

We do AARs after every single evolution. We dissect what we just did to find out what went well and what didn't, what mistakes we made, and what we will correct. We do this constantly and consistently. This is a process of discipline. To be the best in the world, you must continuously evolve, always seeking perfection, never being complacent. The AAR process becomes a way of life.

What's in an AAR?

The structure is pretty simple:

- Goal: what did I/we intend to do

- What happened

- What went right

- What went wrong

- What could be better or What I/we have to fix

AAR Rules

If you are doing an AAR, whether professional or personal, you must set boundaries, so that facts dominate, not feelings. It's not a battle of egos. It's not a time to beat yourself or others up. It is about objectively figuring out what happened, so that you (and your team) can improve.

Dos

- Do be inclusive

- Do be candid and professional

- Do be active (there are no bad ideas)

- Do leave the ego outside

- Do listen and respect

- Do explore disagreements

- Do have an open mind

- Do focus on learning

- Do takeaways and assignments

Don'ts

- Don't dominate the process or bully

- Don't use seniority

- Don't grade

- Don't use as a performance review

- Don't have preconceived prejudices

- Don't get personal

- Don't take it personally

Of course, some of these rules don't apply to an AAR we do for ourselves, but you get the point: *be objective.*

> **AARs include goals, what happened,**
> **what went right, what went wrong,**
> **and what could be better.**

The AAR process permeates the entire SEAL organization. We do it in small teams of two or more. Every deployment cycle, which is six months, the whole force does an AAR, referred to as a Command AAR. During these Command AARs, small "tiger" teams collect the data and assign to-do lists with a completion date. To survive, you must evolve; the most adaptable survive. Every technology company and every market leader that has been disrupted by a technology company knows this. If they are complacent for too long, they become extinct.

> **AARs should be objective, honest, inclusive, respectful, and lead to action.**

AAR Feedback

Doing an AAR and getting feedback is essential to improving, but getting *accurate* and *timely* feedback is critical. Bad feedback is worse than none at all and can anchor bad behaviors into habits or habitudes. Look for input in every part of your life, and don't limit your reviews to your team or yourself. Use technology when you can as well. Fitbit and similar devices are simple examples. When I started meditation, I used a Muse Headband wearable brain sensor, which provided immediate feedback on when the mind became calm and attained an alpha brain waves state. From a meager percentage of calm time, I went to a very high percentage very quickly because I got immediate feedback that I could feel. I can reach that state now quite rapidly. I instill the feedback AAR concept in every part of my life as I monitor my heart rate, blood pressure, steps, body fat, muscle density, and so on.

Learning what you're doing right gives you a DOSE each time, which enables progress and eventually builds good habits.

Time-Out for a Movie, Anyone?

In 2000 the founder of a new struggling company called Netflix approached an industry giant called Blockbuster Video. At the time, Blockbuster was the king of the video rental industry. It had thousands of stores around the country, with millions of customers and massive profits. Netflix wanted to run Blockbuster's online business, and in return, Blockbuster would promote Netflix in its stores around the country. Netflix received a blessing in disguise: they were laughed out of the meeting. By 2010, Blockbuster was bankrupt.

Many case studies have been written about what happened, and a couple of things jumped out at me. The first was this: if you wanted to rent a video, you had to go to a Blockbuster store and get one. Hopefully, the one you wanted was in stock. If not, you settled for another that was available. As you signed the receipt, Blockbuster gave you a date to return the film. The date depended on the popularity of the movie; the newer and more popular the video, the less time you had. If you didn't return the movie on time, Blockbuster penalized you. Every day after that due date incurred additional penalties, often totaling more than the original rental price. Blockbuster made as much as $200 million a year in late fees. This was a significant income stream for them, and they didn't want to give it up. Who would? But as a customer, it angered me to no end, and as soon as Netflix came online, I was happy to jump ship and let Blockbuster go belly-up.

Just like leaders who focus on faults whose employees leave when the opportunity arises, maybe Blockbuster should not have made its revenues by penalizing its customers. Perhaps Blockbuster should have avoided finding (and charging for) faults and instead rewarded the customers who returned movies.

Arrogance was the second problem I saw with Blockbuster. It exhibited considerable complacency and had a fixed mindset with little interest in evolving. Its CEO laughed at Netflix as the meeting ended. Arrogance and ego will hamper your ability to explore other ideas and insulate you from valuable insight into other possibilities—mainly because you think you already know it all. An AAR would have little impact in this environment.

> AARs enable you to adapt to change.
> Species that adapt to change survive.

AARs: Becoming Part of Organizational Culture

I have a program called SEALpreneurship through which I teach mental toughness and GUTS to children as well as adults. During the first summer camp program at San Pasqual Academy, a foster youth high school in southern California, I used the Blockbuster story as an example of evolving and of asymmetrical problem solving. None of the kids knew what Blockbuster was, so Blockbuster *really* is extinct! As a client and friend who is a senior vice president at Microchip Technology, an Arizona semiconductor firm, would say, "You are either green on the vine and growing, or ripe on the vine and dying."

Living our lives focused on faults will destroy our productivity, our business, and our relationships, and even steal our happiness. Some of you may be thinking that people need to be held responsible. Of course, they do! But are we looking to be right, or would we rather be successful? Rewarding victories and focusing on success is not a zero-sum game. You lose nothing by praising others. People and organizations that learn from success create good habits, which evolve into discipline and ultimately become part of the organization's culture. Like a flywheel, the culture of winning gains momentum on its own. Eventually, when you hear, "It's just what we do," then you know it has stuck.

> People and organizations that learn from success create good habits. These habits first evolve into discipline and then become part of the organization's culture.

EXERCISE

Adopt a pays-to-be-a-winner mindset in all aspects of your life. Notice what people are doing right, and let them know it. Praise them for it. This reinforces good habits. Do this consistently and you will see a positive change in behaviors in those around you.

TAKEAWAYS

- Never practice losing. Don't find fault and reinforce a losing message. Focus on successes and wins.

- The DOSE neurotransmitters (dopamine, oxycontin, serotonin, and endorphins) affect focus, sleep, mood, and behaviors.

- Praise, accolades, gratitude, wins (even small ones), and other positive outcomes trigger a steady drip of DOSE.

- Cortisol is triggered by a toxic environment, negative feedback, pain, or stress. Too much cortisol creates more pain or distress, and can lead to health problems.

- DOSE, a little at a time continuously, compounds for you much like compound interest. Likewise, cortisol compounds against you.

- Language is powerful. A single word can give you a DOSE or a disease.

- An After Action Review (AAR) sums up the goals, what happened, what went right, what went wrong, and what could be better. AARs should be balanced, objective, discussed openly, taken seriously, and lead to action.

- Don't just wait for positive (or negative) feedback from others. Do self-reviews and AARs constantly.

You can manufacture motivation if you take the offensive.

- It's not the strongest or the smartest that survives; it is the most adaptable to change. When done right, AARs enable and fuel this adaptation.

- AARs help make winning part of an organization's culture.

7

GETTING PHYSICAL

Build the Body to
Support the Mind

When asked what the most important value in life is, I always answer, "Life." Life is the value. Our health is life, and, like the air we breathe, we often take it for granted until it's gone. To experience the world to the fullest and to accomplish all that we desire, we need to take care of the vehicles that get it done: our bodies. The Latin phrase *mens sana in corpore sano*—"a healthy mind in a healthy body"—speaks to the indelible connection between body and mind, a connection we often ignore.

We evolved a complex and powerful brain to enable high levels of cognitive faculties such as speech, logical reasoning, and problem solving; physical movement and reproduction; and ultimately, our survival. Our bodies are the chassis for our minds. The chassis is the foundation, and a weak foundation makes a vehicle fragile; a little off-road driving stress will

foundation

expose a frail frame, and the vehicle will fall apart. Our chassis is built on four major components: physicality, the physical world, nutrition, and sleep. In this chapter, I show you how to maintain and improve each of these components, and how taken together, they can build the body to support the mind.

> **Our bodies are the chassis for our minds.**

PHYSICALITY: THE BODY AS DURABLE EQUIPMENT

As SEALs, we understand that our bodies are part of our toolkit, that they are weapons in our arsenal, enabling us to accomplish important missions. We live by the expression: "Take care of your gear, and your gear will take care of you." It's not hard to accept this concept when referring to a parachute or rappelling rope because of the apparent danger, but some ignore this idea when it comes to our bodies.

When I was lead instructor for the final phase of BUD/S training, I dropped a student from the program for becoming dehydrated and collapsing on the last land navigation course. Don't get me wrong, this course is not easy. We make the distances long, and each student is required to carry a 45-pound pack to increase the stress. To complete it in the allotted time, a student needs to be either a great navigator or great at carrying heavy loads. At the end, the "A" students are tired, while the "C" students are exhausted.

At first glance, you might think that it wasn't the dropped student's fault because he was carrying a heavy weight over a long distance in a warm, dry climate. After the student was given an IV in the field, he faced a review panel. The student was not a great navigator, so he decided to lighten his load by not taking water. Part of the weight in the pack is a heavy sandbag, which we weigh after the course (we secure the sandbags so students can't empty them and then refill them before they get to the finish line), but the variable part is water. We give students a minimum requirement for water that they *must* take. Most students take more water than required because they know that if their bodies fail, then they fail.

The student was surprised that I dropped him from training. I believe he thought I'd feel sympathy for him, that since he went down medically, his failure would be overlooked, and he would get another chance. But SEALs must adapt and learn quickly—that's one of the necessities of the job. The student was failing in this learning, but that wasn't the main issue. Carrying a minimum amount of water was an order, not a suggestion, so he disobeyed an order. Beyond that, as I explained to him, a SEAL's body is a piece of equipment and part of the mission. Just like any mission-critical piece of equipment, if you neglect it, not only will you fail, but you can also be brought up on charges. Imagine never cleaning your weapon, and it becomes rusted or compacted with dirt and sand, and then the moment you need it, it fails. I explained to him that he must take care of his body, not just because we want him to be well, but because his body is there to accomplish the mission, and he is accountable for its functionality. If it fails him, it fails his team, and if it fails the team, it fails the mission.

> **The body is there to accomplish the mission.**
> **If it fails, it fails the team, and if it fails**
> **the team, it fails the mission.**

When a SEAL's performance is measured, there are seven categories of evaluation. One is "military bearing and character," which includes appearance, conduct, and physical fitness. When an officer is up for promotion, he competes with other SEALs of the same rank and is judged by the senior officers in the community. Each candidate for promotion takes an identical photo with the same camera, wearing the same uniform under the same conditions. When his career is being discussed, his picture is up on the big screen for everyone to see. How we treat our bodies reveals signs of our discipline and self-leadership.

This is certainly true in the SEAL world, but this judgment is prevalent in the business world as well. We may not like it, but we have to acknowledge that people often judge each other on the basis of their appearance, often attributing good qualities such as intelligence or competence—or the opposite—on that basis alone. It's important for professionals, especially leaders, to look the part. A professional appearance that is appropriate to your role is also a sign of respect to those you serve and lead.

Physicality Isn't Just About Going to the Gym

Physicality is a context, an environment, a way of being, not just something you do once in a while. Going to the gym or "getting in shape" is an event, while "physicality" is a way of being that creates the context for going to the gym, eating right, and getting enough sleep. Ideally, the trip to the gym won't be a chore that requires willpower; it will be part of the greater context of physicality—that is, being physical in our lives.

I've been physical all my life, and when I feel like I'm on a downward spiral, I fall back on my physicality as something that makes me successful, motivated, and happy. If I wake up before dawn feeling scared and anxious, as if I was still in combat, I get up and strap on my running shoes. I know the mind drives fear and anxiety, so I take the "inverse evolution" approach: I work my body to soothe my mind. Rain or shine, I get outside and hit the road. Sometimes I run for a couple of hours; other times, I run until I'm finished, meaning as much as I need to. I know that moving and running gives me a DOSE, and quiets my fear and anxiety. I go on the offensive and reconnect with my physicality; it routinely is my therapy. Some days, I go outside and just walk and talk to myself before I start running. The act of going outside is my trigger to run, and once I pull it, the rest just happens. Remember, showing up matters—sometimes it's *all* that matters—and the rest will follow. Find your trigger and pull it.

> **When anxious or nervous, work the body to soothe the mind.**

Seeing the Forrest for the Trees

In 1994 the movie *Forrest Gump* came out, starring one of the greatest actors of all time, Tom Hanks. Hanks played the character Forrest Gump, who starts recounting the story of his life next to a stranger on a park bench. At a very young age, he wore leg braces, and one day, while he was being bullied, his friend Jenny told him to "Run, Forrest! Run!"—and he did. Forrest's braces flew off his legs as he ran; he had found his talent. Although Forrest had a very low IQ, he had a beautiful heart, and running led to enormous accomplishments in his life. As an adult, Jenny, who was recovering from years of drug abuse, came to live with him, but quietly snuck out of his house before dawn without notice. Forrest loved her and was heartbroken, so he did what he knew best, he went running! He became enormously famous because he ran for three years across the country nonstop; he ran until he didn't need to any longer.

On some days, in my mind, I do a Gump run—I run until I don't feel bad. I listen to music as I run a pace at which I can easily focus on my thoughts and coach myself the way I would coach someone else. I don't allow negative movies to play nonstop in my head, and I've become quite good not only at talking to myself but listening to myself as well. The negative feedback loop has stopped.

> **Don't allow those negative movies to play nonstop in your head.**
>
> **Talk to yourself the way a coach would.**

A DOSE of Exercise

If I were a therapist (which I'm not!), I would prescribe a pair of running shoes over anxiety-reducing medication any day. Most studies show that regular aerobic exercise is just as effective as antidepressants to treat mild and moderate cases of depression.

Humans are designed for running. It's nature's way of rewarding and fueling us with a DOSE; the more you run, the greater the DOSE. On the road, I discovered more about who I was and who I wanted to be. It completely changed my state of mind, often, for many hours after my run.

The interesting thing about habits is that they often come with second- and third-order effects. For instance, a habit of over-eating fast food makes you overweight. The second-order effect is that you don't exercise because it's uncomfortable, even painful to move, and your body doesn't feel well. Diabetes and depression can often be a third-order effect. And the cycle continues. Thankfully, this is just as true for good habits like exercise!

Belly Up to the Bars

The operational tempo in Iraq and Afghanistan was intense. We were working as much as 18- to 20-hour days, performing at a high level of planning and execution; war is exhausting in every aspect. Fitness is a SEAL cultural "habit," and it is ingrained in every part of our lives. Even during these long days, we would work out. There was always a pullup bar and a dip bar wherever we went. We brought fitness equipment on deployments. If we were unable to take an hour a day to weight train, every hour or so, we would do a 5- or 10-minute session of max pullups, dips, pushups, air squats, or planks. Often, we kept a board with performance stats to encourage ourselves and each other. Of course, SEALs must stay strong, but that's not the point. This habit of always moving and using our bodies built mental stamina. Moving is a great way to solve problems; even a "walk and talk" can spur ideas you never had. Every time we hit the "bars" (the ones we pull up and dip on), we got a healthy DOSE and were rejuvenated.

> **Take short breaks, go for a brisk walk, or do squats, planks, or any exercise of your choice to get your DOSE.**

Imagine if everyone in an organization took DOSE breaks like we did in combat. Imagine the second and third order of effects: stronger focus, greater productivity, and healthier, happier people. Comfort kills; it kills our motivation and our health. A 2015 CNN article "Sitting Will Kill You, Even if You Exercise," says that prolonged sitting increases the chance of getting Type 2 diabetes, which increases by 90 percent if you sit for prolonged periods like 8 to 12 hours a day.[1] Let's change that, shall we? Go ahead and stand up. Stretch those legs. Move that body. Comfort kills us. Physicality sustains us.

> **Comfort will kill your productivity and kill you.**

LIVING IN THE PHYSICAL WORLD

When we improve our physicality, we broaden our potential experiences in all aspects of life. Physicality is much more than just exercise. The power of physicality to transform us lies in the physical world itself and the nature of our relationship with it.

The first law of thermodynamics states that energy can neither be created nor destroyed; energy can only be transferred or changed from one form to another. When we interact with the natural world, we submerge ourselves in the flow of the physical universe, becoming part of the seemingly endless energy that flows through this universe. As SEALs, we train consistently, around the clock, almost exclusively outside, in nature. For weeks, we live in jungles, forests, deserts, and the Arctic, sleeping on the ground. We spend hours and hours swimming and diving in cold water, exerting ourselves physically, becoming one with the ocean. And yes, cold water does give you a DOSE. People often take cold showers as therapy for mild depression; it also increases alertness and energy. A couple of hours swimming or surfing in cold water will put you in a zone of clarity like nothing else. If you have a big day coming up, try a long cold shower and see how you feel.

One of my fondest SEAL memories is of humping for weeks across Kodiak, Alaska, in snowshoes, carrying a 120-pound pack in deep snow and living in snow caves and tents. We would patrol from sunup to sundown, and by the end of the day, you didn't have a problem sleeping. You were one with nature, getting a heavy DOSE—happy.

Being in the physical world will change your thinking, your judgment, your reasoning. It will transform you and allow you to tap into the natural and instinctive wisdom inherent in you.

New SEAL graduates have an alpha presence that's hard to describe, and it's not just their mental toughness training that's responsible. It's their interaction with the physical world; all the training is outside. The signal that they emit is powerful and affects everyone around them. In the business world, your physical presence and the signs that underlie that presence, signs that may not be immediately obvious, will affect other people. Build that presence by being in the physical world.

The Physical World Isn't Always Good for Us

In 1905 German scientist Robert Koch received a Nobel Prize for his work discovering the causes of diseases such as tuberculosis, anthrax, and cholera. He said: "The day will come when man will have to fight noise as inexorably as cholera and the plague."[2] Think about the noise of today in our cities: car horns, construction, sirens, jets, and more. The vast majority of the sounds we hear are man-made. We didn't evolve hearing what we hear today, and every part of our life is negatively affected by this noise, which contributes to disease, stress, and sleep disorders. On my deployments, all electricity comes from big vehicle-sized generators; you continuously hear them rumbling day and night. When I would get home, I loved to sit outside and immerse myself in silence.

Remember, loud noises are one of the two fears we are born with, so much of this artificial noise we hear triggers our fight-or-flight instinct, killing us slowly. Get some quiet time, preferably in nature, ASAP!

Being "Hard" Isn't Just About Being Muscular

When you see new SEALs in the alpha state, we use a term to describe their physical and mental condition: *hard*. You don't achieve that by being a gym rat—you can't do it indoors, you must be outside. It's a combination of physicality and mental toughness with a connection to the natural world around you. The more you inoculate yourself from straining, the more endurance and tolerance you acquire, and that flows over to other parts of your life.

> Being "hard" is a combination of physicality and mental toughness, with a connection to the natural world around you.

The movie *Rocky IV* was released in 1985, during the Cold War, and was a massive success in America. The American boxer Rocky Balboa fought the Russian Ivan Drago. Although much smaller than his opponent, Rocky was *hard*. The Russian trained with high-tech equipment, used steroids, and had the best team of experts around to transform him, but he trained indoors in a sterile environment. Our hero, Rocky, on the other hand, lived in an isolated cabin and trained outside, in nature, during the Russian winter. He chopped down trees, carried logs, climbed icy mountains—and became *hard* as a result. Of course, Rocky went on to win the fight, and both countries lived happily ever after (well, maybe not!). I know it's a movie, but it does tap into what we intuitively know: being outside in the physical world and *being* physical transforms us in ways we may not understand until we experience it.

NUTRITION: FOOD AS FRIEND (OR FOE)

According to Lieutenant General Mark Hertling, the former Commanding General of U.S. Army Europe and the Seventh Army, one of the biggest threats to our national security might surprise you: it is *obesity*. Obesity and the lack of physicality in our youth have already drained the numbers of potential military-aged recruits. If the trend continues, by the year 2030, 42 percent of Americans nationwide, 50 percent of residents in 39 states, and in some states, as many as 65 percent of children will be obese—not just overweight, but obese.[3]

Obesity has second- and third-order effects, too. It can quickly lead to medical issues and make us sluggish and unable to reap the benefits of exercise, which in turn increases depression and poor self-image, an effect that compounds over time. It's hard to be our best when we feel terrible! We are eating ourselves to death.

When I was redesigning my life after retiring from the SEAL Teams, I knew that I needed to eat and fuel my body for optimal mental and physical performance. I experimented with different nutrition plans and developed a keen awareness of what each did and how it made me feel. By listening to my body and practicing discipline, I've achieved a level of fitness that keeps my body strong and my mind sharp.

Life in the Fasting Lane

I started intermittent fasting two years ago, and I love it! I have clarity, energy, and motivation like I have not had in years. Going 18 hours or more without eating is also a way to delay gratification, which in turn builds discipline. Fasting has been around for thousands of years; its practice is part of every major religion. The *New England Journal of Medicine* has confirmed ancient wisdom: fasting results in "increased stress resistance, increased longevity, and a decreased incidence of diseases, including cancer and obesity."[4]

When you want to change something, you need to change your relationship with it. You need to replace a bad habit with a good one. For example, in some studies, sugar is more addictive than cocaine. You immediately get a DOSE, and the brain craves it. Eating too much sugar will not only make you overweight; it can lead to diabetes, inflammation, depression, anxiety, and even hinder learning and memory. Our bodies aren't designed to be poisoned by sugar, but the average American consumes almost 152 pounds of sugar a year![5] As a society, we need to change our relationship with sugar.

PASS ON, BETTER, LESS

GUTS is not a nutrition book, and even the experts don't agree on what is the best way to eat, but I've experimented a lot, and I know what works for me. I follow what I call the "PASS on, better, less" eating program. I cut down or cut out Processed foods, Alcohol, Sugar, and Starches, while eating "better" (lots of fruits and vegetables) and "less" (cutting portions in half). In a restaurant, I eat half a portion most times. After a while, your stomach will shrink, and you won't be able to eat large meals.

> **Let food be thy medicine and medicine be thy food.**
> **—HIPPOCRATES**

When I've helped people who haven't spent a lifetime using their bodies as a tool, I like to challenge them to learn what it feels like to change an ingrained habit. Try my PASS on, better, less program. Cut down on fried foods, even gluten, and add more vegetables and some pre- and probiotics to your diet. Focus on winning those moments. Don't look at it as a complete lifestyle change at first. Try making small changes to get compounding effects. It's like ending a bad relationship. It's often mentally easier to "take a break" and see how you feel. Distance often gives you clarity. When changing any significant part of our lives, it's often hard to imagine giving up something we're so used to. When you start this separation, in the first couple of weeks, pay close attention to how you feel and think and what you do. What is your mood and motivation? Write it down. Experimentation is essential. Keep what works; discard what doesn't. Celebrate your success as you go! Only you know you like you do, and we all benefit from getting to know ourselves better.

> **We all benefit from getting to know ourselves better.**

Your Gut: The Second Brain

The digestive tract or gut is so crucial to health and overall well-being that there are now countless studies and books calling the gut the second brain. It's connected to the emotional center of the brain, the limbic system. We all know the feeling of butterflies in our stomach when we're nervous, which is the sensation produced by hundreds of millions of neurons lining the gut firing. We've all had a gut feeling. The vagus nerve carries information back and forth between the brain and gut. Also, about 95 percent of the happy hormone, serotonin, is manufactured in the gut. Stress, depression, and anxiety are in a two-way relationship with your gut and your brain, and either organ can cause or be the effect of these issues. A bad mood can produce a lousy gut, and a lousy gut can create a bad mood.[6]

I take care of my gut. I drink kefir and kombucha, eat kimchi, and take pre- and probiotics. When we put premium fuel into our bodies, we get better performance and results. Take care of your gut, and your gut will take care of you.

> **Take care of your gut, and your gut will take care of you.**

SLEEP(LESS) IN CORONADO

Besides cold water and continuous physical exertion, one of the primary tools we use during Hell Week to test the endurance of candidates is sleep deprivation. The students are awake starting Sunday morning and go through Friday afternoon with a total of four hours of sleep *for the week*, give or take a few minutes here and there. By Tuesday morning you can start to observe the drastic effects of sleep deprivation and of physical and emotional exhaustion. By this time, most of the students have quit, and the ones who are left are starting to have difficulty thinking,

solving problems, listening to instructions, and paying attention. They may have hallucinations and often nod off immediately when they stop moving.

Usually by Wednesday or so the students get to stay a little dry and lie down for a snooze, which only takes seconds.
You can see their eyes go into REM sleep almost immediately.
After they get an hour of sleep, we wake them with sirens and
bullhorns, abruptly bringing them back to reality and back to
hitting the freezing surf. For me, this was worse than not getting sleep; it's one of the most painful parts of Hell Week I can
remember.

The ability to sleep—and to function without sleep—is a
key component of the leadership chassis, not just in combat but
also in civilian work and even home life. The barriers to sleep
probably aren't as high as they are in military situations, but
they are there and present a challenge for everyone.

Sleep, Readiness, and Resilience

After almost a decade at war, the SEAL Teams faced some issues that required immediate attention. As the Training and
Readiness Officer, one of the additions I made to readiness was
resilience. We built a program to help combat some of the fa-
tigue that the force was dealing with; the pressure on the teams
was taking a toll. One of the doctors on the permanent medical
staff focused on the body chemistry and sleep of older SEALs
who had been deployed multiple times over the years of fighting. We are all aware of post-traumatic stress disorder (PTSD)
and know that the effects are very harmful and may affect

veterans for life. But SEALs are considerably resilient; their training and preparation help them bounce back quickly in most cases.

One of the factors that stuck out to our doctor was not PTSD per se, it was lack of sleep. A substantial percentage of returning SEALs had significant sleep issues, and I'm one of them. After my second combat deployment, I was assigned another very high-intensity, demanding job, which was essentially seven days a week and required long hours dealing with emergencies and answering to different bosses. To have to go to work at zero dark thirty (3:30 a.m.) and have no idea what crisis would be coming is not a way to decompress. We were severely understaffed and overtasked, and it seemed the wars just kept multiplying. A few months into this job, I received a 10-hour notice for immediate deployment, and once again took off for a different war.

By this time, I dreaded nights because I knew that I would lie there and stare at the clock, waiting for it go off, and that the cycle would repeat night after night. Overseas, in high-consequence environments, you can't afford to waste the few hours you have to sleep, so I kept a big bottle of sleeping pills by my bed. When I was ready to turn in, I took twice the recommended dose and usually got four hours of sleep. We were on vampire hours, operating at night, so sunlight was rare. I'm sure this considerably exacerbated my sleep problems.

When I tried to get off the sleeping pills, I would go as much as 72 hours without falling asleep. So I hit the booze, and although it does work in the short term, it doesn't really do the job. I didn't get proper sleep, just unconsciousness, so the effects of sleep deprivation still lingered, and my level of anxiety remained high.

Our doctor saw sleep deprivation as the most significant health issue we had at the time. Numerous SEALs were stuck in the same cycle as I was, and some were almost psychotic and couldn't function. So instead of medicating SEALs further, the doctor concentrated on the importance of taking the first strike approach to sleep hygiene and educated SEALs on natural supplements to increase sleep efficiency. Although at first he received some pushback from other conventional doctors, his methods significantly helped the force recover. The doctor became so passionate about the importance of sleep that when he retired, he developed his own line of natural sleep aids and now works with professional athletes and lectures worldwide on sleep and wellness.

Get Some Sleep

According to the Centers for Disease Control and Prevention one in three adults get insufficient sleep every night.[7] The effects steal our productivity. Beyond that, exhaustion breeds cowardice; it's easier to give up on important things when we don't have enough sleep and are fatigued. It impairs focus, logical reasoning, complex thought, and judgment, and increases insulin production, among other things.

> **Exhaustion breeds cowardice.**

Sleep is critical to our overall health, well-being, and productivity. It's a time for the body to repair muscle, for the brain to consolidate memory, and for the release of hormones regulating growth, appetite, and other body functions. Ultimately, it is a time to reset our gauges.

Many experts have questioned the efficacy of supplements. I can only speak to my own experience, and, personally, they've worked for me. I take D_3, magnesium (powerful relaxation mineral), Gaba, HTP, B vitamin complex, iron, zinc, a multivitamin, DHEA, and omega-3 fatty acids. Omega-3 fatty acids are not only good for cardiovascular health, they also help improve mood and may have benefits to those suffering from PTSD. At this point, I do not use an alarm clock unless I'm traveling and my sleep cycle is off. I get up naturally at 4:30 or 5 a.m. each morning; if I don't get up naturally, I just go to bed earlier the next night. One other thing I do regularly to contribute to a good night's sleep is *meditate* (as discussed in Chapter 4). You don't need to be sitting in a lotus position in a sari to do it; sometimes I do it in bed. When you meditate, you control your focus and slow down your prefrontal cortex. Sleep comes more quickly when your mind is quiet.

There is so much information available on how to get good sleep; all it takes is a little curiosity and an offensive approach to find what works for you. Be deliberate about sleeping, set the optimal conditions, and make it happen.

Take care of yourself, starting *now*.

EXERCISE

Sit down with a piece of paper and draw four columns representing the four components of your chassis: physicality, the physical world, nutrition, and sleep. Do an honest assessment of your situation in each of these areas in your life and give yourself a score from 1 to 10 (10 is perfect, and you don't need to improve). Write several things down in each category that you can do to improve your scores. Start doing them and building the habits you wish to have. Later I'll talk about goal setting and how to do it so that it STICKS.

TAKEAWAYS

- Our bodies are the chassis for our minds.

- The health of our chassis rests on four major components: physicality, the physical world, nutrition, and sleep.

- Our chassis provides a framework from which our minds can operate. Having a strong chassis improves focus, reasoning, judgment, complex thought, reflex, and readiness.

- Physicality: our bodies are part of our respective toolkits and should be cared for like a piece of gear. Our bodies serve the mind; they are part of the mission and must not fail.

- The body reflects what goes on in our brains; how we treat it reveals signs of our discipline and self-leadership.

- Physicality is a context, an environment, a way of being, not just something you do once in a while.

- The mind drives fear and anxiety, so when anxious or nervous, work the body to soothe the mind.

- Physical world: become one with nature and the outdoors; energy will flow and improve your physical and mental well-being.

- The physical world helps you tap into the natural and instinctive wisdom inherent in you.

- Being *hard* is a combination of physicality and mental toughness with a connection to the natural world around you.

- Nutrition: fuel your body for optimal physical and mental performance.

- Fasting has been proven to be beneficial: it increases stress resistance and longevity, decreases incidence of diseases, and produces clarity, energy, and motivation.

- Try my "PASS on, better, less" diet: little or no processed foods, alcohol, sugar, and starches; lots of fruits and vegetables; and smaller portions.

- Your gut is your second brain, which is closely connected to your first one. Treat it right!

- The ability to sleep—and to function without sleep—is a key component of the leadership chassis, not just in combat but also in civilian work and even home life.

- Sleep works hand in hand with the other components that build a strong leadership chassis. Good physicality, physical world connections, and nutrition help with sleep, and vice versa.

- When it comes to getting good sleep, take an offensive approach to find what works for you. There is a difference between knowing and doing. Be deliberate, set the optimal conditions, and make it happen.

8

STATE OF MIND

The Engine of Performance

It's an amazing sight to watch new graduates of SEAL training and the reaction their parents and loved ones have when they see them for the first time in months. They look at and interact with their sons with awe and amazement—not because they're visibly fitter and stronger but because they sense a difference, a *cerebral* difference. They can tell that he has transformed in ways they don't completely understand, but they know it in their hearts and can feel it.

Likewise, the new SEAL realizes that he has transformed when he interacts with his family and friends for the first time since he started training. He sees the world differently. He can clearly hear for the first time how he's changed, how his conscious and subconscious mind react to the world and those in it. He is more aware, more confident, more perceptive, and more decisive. He moves like an alpha. What has happened?

How has the SEAL training and experience evolved his mind-set and state of mind in new ways?

THE RAS: GATEWAY TO THE CONSCIOUS MIND

The brain is an incredibly complex organ. At any given moment, it receives billions of bits of information, most of which we are unaware of. The conscious mind is like an iceberg: just as most of the ice is underwater, most of the data that the brain receives is in our subconscious, stored for later use. On the other hand, our conscious minds, which contain our thoughts and feelings, are on the surface of our awareness, exposed like the tip of the iceberg.

> **Our bodies tell us what goes into our mouths; what comes out of our mouths tells us what goes on in our minds.**

In our brain stem, there's a bundle of nerves called the reticular activating system (RAS). The RAS is like a bouncer who decides what information is allowed from the subconscious mind into the conscious mind. Our conscious mind is the cool place to be in our everyday lives; every bit of information wants to be there. In my previous book, *First, Fast, Fearless*, I talk about "leader's intent"—how in the world of VUCA (volatility, uncertainty, complexity, ambiguity), leaders can give guidance without knowing all the issues that may be involved. One critical factor that gives leaders intent is a good understanding of what the "end state" looks like. It's not enough to understand what needs to be done, the means. The desired outcome, the end, must also be understood so they know when they have succeeded. Here, the RAS is like a middle manager who must interpret the leader's intent and filter through all the data subconsciously to make decisions on what's important to the "boss"—the conscious mind—and then let that data in. The RAS tends to allow entry to data that validates our beliefs, so it's vital to provide this cognitive "bouncer" with the proper training and inform it of the leader's intent.

Intentions Matter

Intentions have a way of frequently coming true. In 2002 I was taking a course for my master's degree in executive leadership. One of the assignments given by Margie Blanchard, wife of legendary leadership expert and bestselling author Ken Blanchard (*The One Minute Manager* and others), was to write a story about a perfect day 10 years in the future. I wrote about the year I would retire from the SEAL Teams, when I would take my son or daughter with my wife and travel across America for a summer. I dreamed of showing my child this country, the country that I served and for which I fought and am most grateful. At the time, I wasn't married and I didn't have children. Ten years later, in 2012, I did precisely what I'd written: I retired and traveled across the country for the summer with my wife and five-year-old son. A few years later, I was cleaning out some old file drawers and came across the story I had written in class—I had forgotten about it. Intentions matter, even if we are not conscious of the power they have.

Programming the RAS

If we use defensive language repeatedly, like "I'm terrible at x," then our RAS bouncer "hears" it and starts to allow those pieces of data and proof into our conscious mind. When we stop making excuses, and switch our language to "yes," "no," and "I f***ed up," the bouncer will stop allowing excuses into our conscious mind.

Why does traveling transform us? When we immerse ourselves in another culture, we feed the RAS different information, so it starts to change our beliefs or cements them even further, depending on our reaction to our new environment. The conscious mind, as the boss, has to be very deliberate and intentional about its desire to bring the proper clientele into the club. Our thoughts and feelings about people, events, or life in general are our choice, and we can decide what our conscious mind receives, thinks, and feels.

Subconscious in Plain Sight

When I was living in the woods, learning to track like an Apache, I spent days with my face in the dirt, studying tracks. My RAS bouncer knew how important it was to me, so when I left the woods, I could see tracks everywhere, tracks that no one around me could see. This "secret" world was mine alone. Shortly after, I went to Japan to conduct a training mission of Combat Search and Rescue (CSAR) in which I played the bad guy. A pilot was dropped off in the wilderness with a SEAL as his guide and survival expert; that SEAL had lived in the woods, tracking with me, so he knew what I knew about the subject. Pilots plan on the possibility of getting shot down and have to learn to escape enemy hands and evade capture. The world is very different on the ground than it is at 16,000 feet, so even though these pilots are great navigators, they have to practice navigating on the ground to a predetermined spot to get rescued.

Hours after the pilot inserted into the forest, I inserted into the same spot with another SEAL to track him down. Even though the pilot had a considerable head start on me, seven hours later, just before darkness, I caught him. I noticed that the SEAL with me couldn't see the tracks that I could see. I had spent so much time with my face in the dirt that my mind could see subtle disturbances of the earth; my bouncer was doing his job! Since the pilot was carrying his survival gear, the task of seeing the disturbances was like tracking in mud; it just seemed too easy, but not for my partner who couldn't see the tracks. To him, the tracks were like a subliminal message in a movie. His brain hadn't learned to see them yet, but they were there.

Seeing Is Believing—Maybe It Shouldn't Be

Your mind is influenced by what you focus on. Focus commands your time and attention and channels your experiences. These experiences offer proof for your beliefs and strengthen them. Your words become thoughts, thoughts become feelings, feelings become actions, actions become habits, and habits support values and beliefs. They become who you are. In life, we don't always believe what we see; we often see what we already believe.

> **We don't always believe what we see;**
> **we often see what we already believe.**

People are attracted to like-minded people, and nothing has magnified this phenomenon more than social media. Although it has connected people all around the globe, social media has also been one of the most divisive forms of technology created. It's the perfect platform to validate and cement beliefs—right or wrong—that we already have. Just as social media can blind us to reality and crush objectivity, "groupthink" kills organizational creativity.

When Positives and Negatives Don't Attract

I avoid fear-based, toxic, and negative people—complainers, naysayers, and those who see the world as awful and focus on failure. If you know or have ever worked with someone like this, you understand what I mean, and if you don't understand, you might even *be* that person and not know it—*yet*! But that's OK, we can all change; it just takes choice and a little deliberate effort.

When I was regaining my GUTS after retiring from the SEAL Teams, I was angry and saw the world differently than I do now. I saw the world with a fear-based state of mind, and my RAS was sending me proof that the world was dangerous, just like in combat, and that I had to be on alert and look out for threats. This lens was not the one I wanted, so I had to give myself different intentions and proof. I had to set up different filters on my RAS.

One of the first things I did was stop watching the news. I went on the offensive and focused my time and attention on what I wanted. The mind, unlike the body, doesn't come with a liver and kidneys to get rid of toxins, so we have to do it ourselves, intentionally. When you place your focus, time, and attention on your goals and how you want to live, you are practicing self-leadership.

MANAGING YOUR STATE OF MIND

Our state of mind is powerful and determines how we process information and act on it. Our focus, our language, and our chassis all have a direct, two-way cause-and-effect relationship with our state of mind. If we sit on the couch eating junk food and watching cable news all night, using self-defeating language, what is our most likely state of mind? If you exercise regularly, work hard, and just got a big promotion, what is your state of mind? Our state of mind is worth monitoring at all times, it drives us to success or failure.

After multiple deployments to combat, I went to see the doctor for a routine checkup. It struck me as odd that—before even examining me for possible injuries—one of the first things he asked was, "Are you in pain?" At the time, I didn't know that post-traumatic stress disorder (PTSD) is very likely to cause physical pain, especially in the back. The mental pain can actually manifest itself in the body when the anxiety is intense. He was right to ask; my back had seized up and had been awful for a while.

A stressed state of mind can cause hypertension, gut problems, obesity, diabetes, and depression. It can also weaken your immune system, making you more prone to sickness. Too much stress is exceptionally toxic, so we must go on the offensive to mitigate it. But as many retirees know, getting rid of all stress isn't good either. A modest amount of stress is stimulating, exciting, and fulfilling. We need a balance.

Dealing with Toxicity

Stress can come in small doses from a wide variety of sources, or it can come in large waves from a few or even a single source. The style employed by your manager or leader can cause enormous stress. Think of the typical insecure manager who is incompetent, inconsiderate, secretive, and uncommunicative, among other things. Got one in mind? I knew you would. An *Inc.* magazine article cites a recent study that found that employees are as much as 60 percent more likely to suffer a heart attack if their bosses have these traits.[1] We know everyone despises toxic leaders, but they actually can kill you!

When I started consulting and teaching leadership, I worked with a rather large company, which may have had the worst environment I've ever experienced. In a room filled with a couple dozen senior leaders, it became very apparent that everyone in the room was terrified of the boss. Their language exposed his toxicity; it was thick in the air and I could feel it. At one point, he made an appearance, and as he approached, the tension in the room could be cut with a knife. His posture was aggressive, he didn't smile, and he completely failed to engage with his senior leaders. If he did talk to them, it was about what he expected them to get from the leadership training. Indeed, the looks on their faces were similar to those of high-level generals in the North Korean Army when addressed by their Supreme Leader.

This toxic behavior and suffocating fear had woven itself throughout the organization, resulting in self-preservation, backstabbing, and other forms of detrimental behavior. At one point, one senior leader looked across the room and apologized to one of the other leaders, with tears in his eyes, because he had thrown him under the bus to keep from suffering the boss's wrath, and he felt guilty. These people were in a tough position: do they quit, try and get him fired, sabotage him—*what?* It was clear that they had become the effect that was caused; they were in an awfulizing state of mind. The downward spiral in negativity and toxicity undermined this organization's ability to perform as a can-do, positive team. The road forward would be difficult without a major change in leadership and/or a major change in mindset.

If you are in a similar situation, you may not be able to control the former, but you can certainly control the latter. Think positive as much as you possibly can and realize that it's not about *you*. Don't let the toxicity and fear penetrate your psyche and change *you* and your *state of mind*. Look for opportunities to gently suggest better ways of communicating to the boss that will result in better outcomes. Do not frame this as criticism, but as a way to be a better leader. If you have direct reports, protect them from this toxicity; be the shield that prevents this from cascading down to them. Every situation is different, but know that hardship and adversity always present opportunities for growth, so focus on how this can make you a better leader and a better human being.

> **Don't let toxicity change your state of mind. Instead, use it as an opportunity to do something positive and grow.**

Perception, Response, and Self-Control

It's easy to allow our circumstances to control our state of mind and ultimately steal our happiness. Happiness is not determined by success in life, rather, success is determined by happiness. Dr. Viktor Frankl, bestselling author of *Man's Search for Meaning*, lived through the Holocaust in a concentration camp and reportedly said: "Between stimulus and response there is a space. In that space is our power to choose our response. In our response lies our growth and our freedom." How we respond is our *choice*; only we can make it. We must be deliberate and intentional.

> **Between stimulus and response there is a space. In that space is our power to choose our response. In our response lies our growth and freedom.**
> **—DR. VIKTOR FRANKL**

Realize that everyone has something in their lives driving their state of mind at any given moment. No time in the recent past provides as good an example as the Covid-19 pandemic. The severe ramifications of the virus triggered twin fears, for our health and for our financial well-being, plunging most people in a state of mind they had never had before—defensive, tentative, afraid to do anything or interact with anyone. People who were typically confident and very much in charge of their lives felt powerless and helpless. Normal patterns of human and business interactions were widely disrupted. Particularly during this episode, but more generally, if more subtly, in "normal" times, we get a sense of how others are feeling based on how they are behaving. When negative behavior is observed, empathy will help you control your emotional response. Focusing on others and their state of mind will help prevent your ego from being triggered and *your* state of mind from being changed. It's all about perception, response, and self-control.

> **When emotional, restraint is strength.**
> **Controlling your emotions is mastery of self.**

When State of Mind Controls You

Our experiences help our RAS filter information to create an intuition or "sixth sense" in combat. When I would deploy to a hazardous city, I'd go out with the soldiers who had long been there patrolling the streets and had lived through it. Several times these soldiers would slam on the brakes or cross the median seemingly out of nowhere. They could "feel" something and knew to react to it. Their sixth sense was sending them a signal. Their subconscious minds had collected all of that data and sent them a feeling—not a conscious report—and they reacted. Those who survive patrolling those streets have extreme focus, and they develop and listen to their intuition.

There is one problem: when you come home from active duty, all of this "hazard" information filling your mind becomes useless—it (fortunately) isn't needed in ordinary life—but the mind doesn't stop doing what you needed it to do for so long. Driving down the street, every roadside object can look like a threat because, in combat, a pile of rocks might be a marking device to set off an IED when your vehicle approaches. Traffic going at a high rate of speed can be perceived as an immediate threat as well. Your state of mind is hypervigilant, and it is possible to overreact. What is most important is to understand how the past has altered your state of mind. Recognizing that is the first step toward healing.

Over time, in combat, fear turns into paranoia, anger, and hatred. Those feelings create a state of mind, which then shapes how we see the world, our day-to-day life, and our future. We become the effect being caused, and we aren't likely to be happy or successful.

You don't need to be in combat to develop a fear- or negativity-based state of mind. This belief system causes you to continuously ruminate and awfulize, which in turn anchors any negative "proof" in your subconscious mind. This is not a good place to be.

> There is nothing either good nor bad,
> but thinking makes it so.
> **—WILLIAM SHAKESPEARE, *HAMLET***

Taking Control of State of Mind

How do we control our state of mind? As a good self-leader, one of the best methods is to take care of our chassis because how we feel overall affects our state of mind. If our bodies feel awful, are in pain, or are not working well, it negatively affects our state of mind. If we don't sleep and are in a state of physical and mental exhaustion, which breeds cowardice, it becomes easy to give up on our goals and what we want out of life. However, if we are being physical, eating well, taking care of our gut, and DOSEing ourselves regularly, then we feel better. Emotions drive motion, and conversely, motion drives emotion.

It's also critical to recognize when past events—prior conflicts with others, terrible mistakes, unfortunate experiences—may have altered your state of mind. If that is the case, the next step is to pick a particular event and reframe your internal language around it. With almost any experience in your past, there is a glass half empty and a glass half full—negative and positive—aspect to it. Go on the offense, and focus on the glass half full.

> **Emotions drive motion; conversely, motion drives emotion.**

Although Hollywood is full of fantasy and make-believe, some of the most convincing actors of all time practice a technique called "method acting," by which they transform into the characters that they want to be. They don't fake it until they make it; they do it until they become it. They lose themselves in the character's life, and they study everything about the character. They learn to move, talk, and, ultimately, think and feel like the character. They gain or lose weight to get a better understanding of how the person must have felt in his or her body. The portrayals of Abraham Lincoln by Daniel Day-Lewis and Mary Todd Lincoln by Sally Field in Steven Spielberg's film *Lincoln* serve as fine examples.

So does Bradley Cooper's portrayal of SEAL sniper Chris Kyle in the movie *American Sniper*. To prepare for the role, Cooper gained as much as 40 pounds of muscle, perfected a Texas accent, and learned how to shoot sniper rifles from former Navy SEAL sniper Kevin Lacz. Interestingly, Cooper said in an interview he had to change his complete body chemistry to play Chris. Cooper knew that by transforming into Chris, he would develop the state of mind of the most successful sniper in American history. In a *Los Angeles Times* article, Cooper recalled that "he didn't really leave me." The reporter noticed him scanning the room just as he would have if he were actually Chris Kyle or another person used to being in dangerous places.[2]

The point: We *can* change our state of mind; it's our choice. We can work both ways, using our minds and bodies to drive each other like a balanced machine.

EXERCISE

Pay close attention and focus on your state of mind. If you're in a negative or fearful state of mind, practice changing it to the state you desire to be in. Change your external and internal language to stop awfulizing. Before critical events or interactions, take charge of your state of mind. Do not allow it to take charge of you. Be the cause of the effect, not the effect that was caused.

TAKEAWAYS

- The reticular activating system (RAS) acts as a gateway between the subconscious and conscious mind. It works as a cognitive "bouncer," filtering data from the subconscious and controlling what enters the conscious mind. It is the source of our intuition.

- RAS inputs can be quite obvious or quite subtle, like animal tracks in a forest.

- Your words become thoughts, thoughts become feelings, feelings become actions, actions become habits, and habits support values and beliefs; they become who you are.

- Fear spreads easily, and sometimes is just a matter of seeing what we already believe instead of seeing things objectively.

- Our focus, our language, and our chassis all have a direct, two-way cause-and-effect relationship with our state of mind.

- Our state of mind is powerful and determines how we process information and act on it.

- Negativity often breeds negativity and can lead to a toxic environment, which feeds on itself and suppresses creativity, initiative, productivity, teamwork, and action.

- Dealing with toxic environments means (1) realizing it's not about you; (2) focusing on the positive; (3) gently suggesting to the boss better ways of communicating that will result in better outcomes; and (4) not letting it change your state of mind.

- The mind, unlike the body, doesn't come with a liver and kidneys to get rid of toxins, so we have to do it ourselves, intentionally.

- According to Dr. Viktor Frankl, "Between stimulus and response there is a space. In that space is our power to choose our response. In our response lies our growth and our freedom."

- Success does not lead to happiness; happiness leads to success.

- To improve your state of mind, take care of the chassis. Get physical, eat right, sleep right, and DOSE yourself regularly. Recognize the experiences that might have harmed your state of mind, and deal with them objectively.

- Emotions drive our motion; our motion drives our emotions.

9

INTO THE COCKPIT

Piloting Your
Body/Mind Machine

About a year after the start of the Iraq war, I found myself on foot, moving through the streets of Baghdad at about zero dark thirty. I was in the northeastern area, referred to as Sadr City. The enemy owned the city, and improvised explosive devices (IEDs) were everywhere. That night, we had to leave our vehicles several blocks away from the target building because we knew it was full of enemy combatants. As I exited the vehicle, I remember looking down at my feet and seeing what appeared to be an IED with wires hanging out; I was straddling it! We began to move toward the target, and as I snuck through the destroyed streets, I walked right up to a group of Iraqis sitting beside a fire burning in a barrel. Although I was equipped with body armor, lasers, and conventional weapons, they didn't seem to be at all alarmed that I was there. They just stared at me. At this time in the war, we had no idea who was an enemy or who was harmless. It's easy to believe that everyone you encounter, especially at zero dark thirty, will attack you, and everyone is a threat. Somehow I didn't feel that way, but what I *did* feel was a sense of déjà vu. I felt as if I had been there before and that I already knew the outcome. I didn't as much think it as *feel* it. I experienced a deep sense of calm and certainty. What was happening?

Before I deployed on this mission, I spent time with the group that had come back, and they not only covered tactics but also told stories of what it was like. I wanted to know what the streets looked like, what they smelled like, and what I would experience. Remember, when we are facing the unknown, our minds tend to fill that void by awfulizing. My fellow Special Operators told me that it was fairly common for the locals, who had no electricity, to huddle around a fire pit to stay warm and protect their neighborhoods. I had seen this situation hundreds of times in my mind; I had experienced it over and over, so I knew how I would react to it.

At the center of the feeling of calm and certainty was that remarkable organ, that "cockpit" for all my thoughts, emotions, fears, actions, and reactions—my brain.

THE SEEMINGLY INFINITE POWER OF THE MIND

The human brain makes up only about 2 percent of our total weight, but it consumes almost a quarter of our energy. Most people allow it to operate on autopilot, without deliberate intent. Our chassis affects the performance of our brain, but it is not the only influence. By controlling how we think and what we think, we control the destiny of our lives. We bring our A (alpha) game to every situation because we are in control and have a choice; we are the cause of the effect, not the effect that was caused.

> **By controlling how we think and what we think, we control the destiny of our lives.**

Mind over Muscle

In 2004 clinical physiologist Guang Yue wanted to know if visualizing was enough to increase strength without actually performing an exercise. He devised an experiment with two tests and divided the subjects into four groups, two groups per test. The first test involved finger strength. One group tried to strengthen their finger muscles by doing finger exercises; the other group only visualized doing the exercises. The second test involved arm strength. One group attempted to increase arm strength through visualization alone, while the other group did nothing at all. The experiment ran for 12 weeks, five days a week for 15 minutes a day.

The group that did the finger exercises saw an improvement of 53 percent in finger strength, but the exciting finding was that the groups that visualized doing the exercises saw a 35 percent improvement in finger strength and a 13.5 percent improvement in arm strength! Imagine that! Well, as a kid who idolized Arnold Schwarzenegger, I did imagine that, and so did Arnold.

In his book *The New Encyclopedia of Modern Bodybuilding*, Schwarzenegger said: "I also used a lot of visualization in biceps training. In my mind, I saw my biceps as mountains, enormously huge, and I pictured myself lifting tremendous amounts of weight with these superhuman masses of muscle." It was as if his mind was willing his muscles to grow stronger and bigger. Arnold was onto something. All bodybuilders understand that to maximize growth, you must focus your mind's eye on the specific muscle and be "inside it" to engage it fully. What's interesting is that neuroscientists have found that the same neuron circuits fire in the brain when performing an action and merely visualizing performing the action.

> **In my mind, I saw my biceps as mountains.**
> **—ARNOLD SCHWARZENEGGER**

The power of the mind is also evident in the phenomenon of the "placebo effect," in which people expecting a beneficial effect experience that effect after taking a placebo, a substance or treatment designed to have no therapeutic value, such as sugar pills or saline injections. Placebos work on symptoms that are modulated by the brain, like the perception of pain. Visualizations of living a clean and healthy life, eating well, exercising, being in nature, and other positive habits have also been shown to improve the placebo effect. We believe it works, so it works.

MIND AS COCKPIT: COMMAND CENTER, SIMULATOR, TIME MACHINE

Humans are the only animal that can imagine, react emotionally, and create a state of mind. We can awfulize, get scared of the future, and even get depressed, or we can focus our thoughts on the potential we have and get excited and exhilarated for the future. We have the ability to control our emotions and our state of mind.

> **We have the ability to control our emotions and our state of mind.**

If our bodies are our chassis, our state of mind is our engine, and our emotions are the fuel that drives us. Our mind is our cockpit. It is the command center for all that we do. Beyond that, it's unique in that it serves as a simulator in which we can practice and a time machine in which we can travel.

Science fiction is an excellent indicator of the potential for human imagination and visualizing the future. The comic *Dick Tracy*, which debuted in 1931, had its main character using a two-way wrist communication device. Years later, that character's communication device inspired Martin Cooper at Motorola to invent the first cell phone. Today we have smartphones that enable us to video chat, access all public information the world has to offer, navigate, and even monitor our home from across the globe. After visiting the 1964 New York World's Fair, science fiction author Isaac Asimov predicted the rise of cars with robot brains; today we have self-driving vehicles.[1]

Our minds operate in past, present, and future. They can go on or off autopilot (where we spend a lot of time). We allow our minds to jump between the past, present, and future without having our hands "on the wheel." But to deal with fear, manufacture motivation, and maximize success, you must have a deliberate plan and tools to control and shape your mind.

Training *Your* Mind

Exploring mind training is like spelunking into caves where no one has ever been. It's a little scary, but also intriguing. We control the limitations to our own change and success; we just need enough faith and curiosity to start exploring.

Imagine sitting in the cockpit of your favorite sports car and looking down at the gauges and controls on the panel, designed to monitor and race this vehicle to its maximum potential. I use the race car analogy to make mind training more tangible and applicable to different aspects of your life. There are specific tools for you to use. These include intent, the chassis, state of mind, offensive first strike language, visualization, our senses, and breathing. These are all precheck items we need to describe and prepare before our mind-training evolution.

Intent: Start with the End in Mind

Before we start, we must understand the intent of what we are doing: what is the outcome that we seek? As a leader, when I state a leader's *intent*, I include the *purpose, key tasks*, and *end state*. It gives subordinates enough context to act independently, that is, to exercise initiative when unanticipated opportunities or constraints arise or when the plan they are executing is no longer relevant. The *purpose* gives a broader understanding of their efforts against big-picture objectives, such as eliminating a terrorist threat, or in business, gaining market share by making a product more competitive. It gives a strong sense of why they are doing what they are doing; it gives clear intent. How do you articulate that purpose?

The second part of a leader's intent incorporates *key tasks*. These are the critical actions that must be done along the way. The last and most critical part, the *end state*, explains what success looks like—it's a clear mental picture of victory. As a leader, delegation isn't about making assignments. It's about sharing an intended outcome.

> **As a leader, delegation isn't about making assignments, it's about sharing an intended outcome.**

Understanding the intent also triggers our reticular activating system (RAS) and sets it up to filter inputs according to what we seek to do. Down the road, our RAS will pull the pieces together in ways that we never imagined. It will assemble information in the context of what our end state is.

Chassis: Get Your Body Ready

Before we climb into the cockpit simulator to start mind training, we should take inventory of the state of our chassis. To prepare, it helps to generate a DOSE (dopamine, oxytocin, serotonin, and endorphins) and modify your state of mind. You can do this by exercising, being in nature, healthy eating, and getting good sleep.

State of Mind: Keep Positive

Our state of mind can dictate the outcome of our lives. When I plan for my goals, I always make it a point to be in a positive state of mind. If I'm planning to write my next book, I think about all the positive outcomes—the successful business transaction, the satisfied readers, the completion of a long-contemplated task—which then gets me into an excited and curious state of mind prior to putting pen to paper. You should never plan the future in a negative state of mind *unless* that is your intent. If you do, you will bring that emotion with you into the future, and that emotion will attach itself to the future event. But what may be considered a "negative" emotion can sometimes be useful. For example, for combat, I trained to be aggressive and very deliberate. Sometimes before going into a meeting to give a very unpopular order, I would get into a very stoic, stern, and decisive state of mind. If opposed, I had the right state of mind to quash the opposition.

Timing is also important. It's generally not a good idea to do something that may release a lot of negative energy right before doing something that requires positive energy. What do I mean? Suppose I go to the Department of Motor Vehicles and wait in line for two hours, only to find out that they lost my paperwork and I would have to come back the next day—that would impair my state of mind. I wouldn't want to go home and start mentally rehearsing my next speaking engagement just then. If I did rehearse my speech that way, my default emotion might very well be anger, which would show on stage.

Language: The First Strike

Language is key to our success because language creates visual images and thus creates or stimulates thoughts. We must control it to control our outcomes.

Some people have difficulty being their own best coach. They often think that what they say to themselves is a lie; they don't feel authentic. Obviously, this is one of those self-fulfilling loops that's easy to get in and will sabotage our evolution and progress in life. During this self-talk time, it may be helpful to speak in the third person, the way I was taught to do in Officer Candidate School (OCS)—"Hiner can run a four-minute mile. Easy!" Imagine coaching someone you have a lot of faith in, but who doesn't have a lot of faith in herself—*yet*! Coach yourself with language that you would use if you were coaching someone else, putting as much of a positive spin as possible so as not to perpetuate self-doubts. Language is a tool you use to facilitate change, to get you where you want to go.

Visualization: In Sight, It Must Be Right

The brain receives as much as two-thirds of its information from sight, dominating the senses. In fact, neurons dedicated to visual processing take up as much as 30 percent of the cortex. Visualization is more than just a lens with which to record the world; it provides an almost instant understanding. Imagine a pink elephant juggling bowling pins, wearing a black vest, smiling, and looking at you while standing on a ball. You've never physically seen this image before, but your mind just did, guided by words. Visualization can create experiences that the mind doesn't distinguish much from "real experiences." If you visualize yourself doing a task, it will create mental pathways that, over time, will help enable you to achieve it.

Senses: Passing the Smell Test and Others

When mind training, we must bring our senses to bear to maximize the benefits. Although sight brings the most information to the brain, smell is unique in its own way. Smell bypasses the thalamus and goes straight to the limbic brain via the olfactory nerve. This "lizard" brain is connected to the amygdala and hippocampus, and plays a significant role in our mood, memory, behavior, and emotions. We've all experienced how a smell can instantly take us back to an emotion-laden memory. The smell of gun oil or explosives is comforting and satisfying to me, the same way the scent of horse manure might evoke happiness in a horse lover—something most people may not understand. The scent of a fighting gym is like home to some, and utterly disgusting to others. Every time I smell leather and fresh-cut grass, it brings me right back to playing baseball as a young kid, dreaming of becoming a Major League ballplayer.

Breathing: Take Your Breath Away

Although we breathe continually all day every day, it's one of the most overlooked tools that we have to help change our state of mind and overall wellness. There is much to be explored with breathing, but the main thing to understand is how breath effects physicality, and ultimately our mood. Here I will focus on two broad forms of breathing, *deliberate diaphragm* and *hyperventilation* breathing. If we want to calm down and engage our parasympathetic nervous system (the opposite of the sympathetic fight-or-flight system), we breathe deeply while engaging our diaphragm. I use the simple technique, the "4×4 method," breathing deeply in through the nose with a four-count, and then out through the mouth with a four-count. The stomach goes out, forcing the diaphragm to contract, and the chest remains still; this is often called stomach breathing and deep breathing. It's a little awkward in the Western world because a flat stomach is desirable, so we naturally hold our stomach in and breathe shallow through our chest, not our stomach. Breathing shallow through our chest, which most people do all day, can actually engage our sympathetic nervous system (fight or flight). During mind training, it helps to engage my sympathetic nervous system to spark enough anxiety to help snap me into focus. Generally speaking, I do this by hyperventilating for a short period, which manipulates the level of CO_2 in the bloodstream and ultimately triggers the sympathetic response. It's an inverse cause and effect and gets me a little hyped up.

GETTING THE MIND READY:
A PREDEPLOYMENT REGIMEN

During predeployment training, a SEAL Team will repeat all the training they have done in the past to sharpen their skills in all forms of warfare. Before every block of training, like Close Quarter Battle (CQB), I would set a goal to be the best shooter and outperform everyone. The rivalry between officers and enlisted SEALs is a constant and acts as a healthy way of keeping the bar high on standards and performance. On the weekend, or several days before starting the particular training, I would begin mental rehearsals to clear the cobwebs and get a head start on refreshing my skills. Most skills you learn are perishable, and over time they diminish, so it's important to always revisit and sharpen them.

We have an expression I learned early on and live by: "It takes a shooter to lead a shooter," meaning as a leader, you better be at your best to earn the respect of those you lead. This is why I set the goal to outperform everyone else. If I succeeded, I never said a word. I just let the results speak for themselves. Plus, coming out of the gates a little ahead on each block of training establishes a halo effect that transfers well across many disciplines and builds your team's confidence in you.

Is There a "G" in "Team"?

When you appear to be a genius at something, people don't feel threatened or inferior; they just believe you have a God-given talent and have extreme confidence in you. This halo effect goes a long way toward building effective teams. In her book *Grit: The Power of Passion and Perseverance,* author Angela Duckworth includes this quote from philosopher Friedrich Nietzsche: "Our vanity promotes the cult of the genius. For if we think of genius as something magical, we are not obliged to compare ourselves and find ourselves lacking. . . . To call someone 'divine' means: 'here there is no need to compete.'"

INTO THE COCKPIT

Different methods of mind training exist, but personally I like to visualize myself in a cockpit where I can see gauges that represent points of performance like speed or heart rate in a run, tools like a steering wheel to adjust direction, and other tangible items I can control and manipulate to respond to different situations. Next I'll describe two scenarios to show how it works and how to build your own cockpit simulator to train in the past, present, and future. Scenario 1 is a cockpit in the present: you are in the event and controlling focus, minimizing awfulizing, and maximizing performance as you go. Scenario 2 is a simulator "time machine" in which your focus is on a future action. It involves creating the mental pathways you desire when the event does occur.

Scenario 1: An All-Out Run to the Finish

As I've described, most days I go out for a run, which I call a "jam." Typically, I don't push my limits of speed. Instead, I put myself on autopilot, running at a comfortable pace while focusing on what I'm doing currently or problem solving a particular situation. I'm sure my neighbors think I'm nuts because I talk to myself out loud about whatever I'm working on at the time. For example, if I have an upcoming speaking engagement, I rehearse the concepts. During these sessions, my RAS pushes out a lot of information to me, and I see how all the dots connect. These runs are not just for fitness. I use them to think things through. They're a form of therapy for me that I love. But I also happen to be very competitive. I love a competition, and it's really hard for me not to engage when the moment presents itself.

I live in Southern California, and a lot of people here compete in triathlons. They compete around the world and train year-round. I usually go out for an autopilot run, but when I see one of these "tri-guys" in their body tights, weighing in at about a buck fifty, I know the race is on.

I immediately take myself off autopilot and grab the wheel, which is my focus. I'm no longer out there for a therapy session. I'm in the present, and it's game on! At this point, I imagine my gauges lighting up, just like in a movie when a pilot must snap to attention when something happens in a plane. Immediately, I come up with a plan to win. I know how far I plan to race him (or her). If I know it's one mile to my turn-off, then I'm in a one-mile race. I'm 30 feet behind him, and I know he knows I'm there because I can feel him pick up his pace. Competitors do not like anyone running up behind them and passing them, especially someone who's not built like a runner but more like a linebacker, as I am. The performance points in my mind become imaginary gauges and controls, which in turn, direct my focus, effort, speed, explosive exhalations, body limpness, and stride, among others. I systematically switch from gauge to gauge in my mind to monitor all points of performance and to maximize my output.

I start off with a gradual increase in speed, knowing how much distance I have to cover. I know how much effort I have to put in to maintain my speed for that distance. I start to "pre-breathe," meaning I overbreathe deeply, focusing on explosive exhalations rather than inhalations. These exhalations get CO_2 out of my system and flood it with oxygen, preparing my body for the assault. When I explode my breath out, I imagine getting all the CO_2 out of my lungs, opening up space for the oxygen I need to fuel my legs. In my mind I'm monitoring the gauges and talking to myself, just as I would if I was coaching someone else:

> RPMs are up near the red, I'm good, going slightly downhill, longer stride and speed up, the RPMs are dropping, keep it at the red and push it! Explosive breath, relax the body, hands limp, explosive breath, here comes a small hill, overbreathe now, explosive breath, get ready for the hill!

I'm monitoring my body and my opponent. "Hitting the hill, short stride, chop steps, back down on RPMs, explosive breath, now I'm on him!" At this point, I'm breathing deeply, focusing on exploding air out of my lungs. I take the RPMs up in the red by exerting more effort and speeding up to where I can really feel it burning. I take it a little bit higher, right where I know I can hold it for the short distance I have left. Now my language shifts and becomes more aggressive because as a coach to myself, I want to get fired up for the finish line like people do when their racehorse is coming down the stretch. I'm continuously monitoring my gauges, never allowing myself to focus on the discomfort my body is feeling.

If you ever listen to pilots when they're dealing with a flight emergency, they are calm and matter-of-fact, checking off their gauges and going through their procedures just like they did in training. They are not in a panic; they are in control. They don't focus on dying. They focus on what needs to be done, and they do it with the same precision they mastered in the simulator. In times of extreme stress, we don't necessarily rise to the occasion; we fall back on our training.

As I fly past the runner, I do it vigorously. I'm running at top speed, and I can feel the runner chasing me, taking the bait. I go through my mental gauges quickly:

> Explosive breath, turn up the RPMs in the red, limp arms, long stride, explosive breath, turn it on, put the f***ing hammer down, run motherf***er, run! Hammer down, hammer down, long stride, turn up the RPMs, let it run, let it run!

I'm doing nothing but focusing on keeping up my speed and effort, but right before the end, I have what I call a "nitro button," a set of trigger words ingrained in me in BUD/S training long ago that give me the boost of emotional energy to take me past my own limitations: "Hammer down, hammer down, HOOYAH, motherf***er!" When I go through this dialogue and finish it with the trigger phrase, I get goosebumps. I reach deep inside and can feel the emotional energy finding another gear that I usually don't have, pushing me forward. I'm running on pure heart.

If you'll notice, as I'm doing this, I am constantly focused on my gauges, checking one point of performance after another, making the necessary adjustments to maintain my maximum output, never allowing myself to focus on the discomfort or pain. My language is deliberate and controlled.

Keeping your hands on the steering wheel (focus) is critical to being in the moment and not allowing fear and discomfort to take over. If you're not focused, they can fill your thoughts and derail your self-talk, and you never get to the "hammer down" push to the summit. Other distractions—the naysayers and fault-finders at work or the cell phone in your teenager's hand as you try to have a serious parent-to-child discussion—may threaten, but keeping an eye on the gauges helps you stay focused, and others will respond to that focus.

Such focus also helps you manage the waiting times and anxiety before an event, which can often be the worst period of time in the whole sequence, as combat veterans and public speakers alike will tell you. Waiting to go into combat is by far the most stressful part of combat because of the empty void in front of you. It's easy to lose focus and start to awfulize the future. You begin to visualize the worst-case scenario, creating an Oscar-winning horror movie in your own mind. When you allow your mind to focus on pain or discomfort, it will magnify and grow. That's when the loss of willpower creeps in and quitting happens.

Scenario 2: Prepping for Close Quarters Battle

Elite athletes understand the power of mental training for future events, but mental training is not just for physical performance. It's for anyone who wants to improve, reduce the fear of the future, and motivate herself to do whatever it is she wishes to do. It's a way of practicing an event without physically doing it. This training is how we create the feeling of déjà vu for activities that we haven't yet done. It makes the future familiar, which reduces our fear and makes us more comfortable with the unknown, which is not really unknown to us after training extensively in a simulator.

In 1977 Natan Sharansky, a computer specialist, was arrested in the USSR for spying and spent nine years in solitary confinement. A successful chess player all his life, he claimed that chess saved his life while he was in prison. He didn't have a chess set or a partner. Instead, he played mental chess all those years, against himself. "I might as well use the opportunity to become the world champion," he quipped. He was released in 1986, and in 1996 he beat world chess champion Garry Kasparov. Obviously, his mental training during those years paid off.

One of the most challenging and useful skills SEALs train for is CQB. Some of the compounds we secure are as big as a cargo ship or shopping mall, which may take hours, or as small as a one-room shack. The intent of CQB is to clear the structure to capture or kill combatants, get intelligence, seize the ship or structure, and/or save hostages. There are many points of performance involved in CQB, and it's considered one of the baseline skill sets we have to master as most direct action missions involve entering a structure. How you perfect CQB will determine your success and whether you live or die. Just like the Chief who was shot 27 times, you will fall back on your level of training.

Being a surgical shooter is one critical piece of the mission. It involves being able to shoot your primary (rifle) and secondary (pistol) weapon in a reasonably close range while moving with extreme accuracy and speed. At times, you may take a headshot while moving in a dark room, right by the head of a noncombatant or hostage, so the difference between success and failure can be inches. We have an expression we live by: "You can't miss fast enough to win a gunfight," meaning you must hit your target quickly.

The other huge piece of the mission is the flow through the building, which begins with a perfect two-person room entry, and escalates into an assault force, moving through a large structure as if it was a choreographed dance. With each room entry the scenario changes; you can never predict the size and shape of the rooms, the hazards, the number of combatants you encounter, and more. Flow happens after a team has been training together for a while, and the entire team starts to have one shared consciousness. They begin to move like a single organism, covering all angles, picking up fields of fire, predicting the next moves, and so forth. This is where your RAS and the subconscious mind are active before your conscious mind can cognitively think about the next step. In some sense, these are "instincts," but instincts that we can build.

During CQB you must dominate the angles; it's all about the geometry. Whoever wins the angles wins the fight. You know you're getting into the flow when you see the angles, and you're able to predict the size, shape, and hazards in the next room so you know where to put yourself, whether you're in a combat situation or not, after the training. Your RAS brings these calculations to your attention, and you can't help but see the world through the CQB lens. You can also use a simulator to accelerate this inside-the-cockpit response with deliberate training.

When I climb inside my mental simulator, my intent is to master perfect shooting techniques and economy of motion, so that there are no wasted movements in any aspect of the assault. That applies to my body position when I'm shooting and moving, how I manipulate my weapon, and how I walk or run inside the target building. Every movement needs to be exact, nothing wasted. I want to move in a synchronized flow with the team.

PREPARING TO TRAIN THE MIND

I normally do mind training after working out because I want my body to be energized and the chassis warmed up. If I don't have time for a full workout, I do shorter exercises, such as shadow boxing, jumping jacks, or breathing exercises, to give myself a quick DOSE to achieve the desired state of mind.

Start with Your Nerves on Alert

Most people think that they should be calm during this training. Not me. I don't want to be too calm. I want to be in a heightened state to draw my focus tight on what I'm doing. For CQB I want to be in a surgical, steely-eyed alpha state of mind. Not emotional, not amped up like a football player before kickoff, but deliberate and decisive, like a pilot flying through bad weather. Hyperventilation is one quick hack to get my sympathetic nervous system engaged. I lie on my back, breathe deeply and rapidly, 30 to 50 breaths, exhale all of the air out of my lungs, and then hold my breath for as long as I can. I take in a deep breath, hold it for 10 seconds, and repeat the process. I usually do this three times. SEALs learn this and other breathing techniques to be able to endure cold water for long periods.

Wim Hof, a Dutchman who has set numerous Guinness World Records for withstanding extreme temperatures, made the technique famous. When you hyperventilate, you rid your body of CO_2 and saturate it with oxygen. When you shift and hold your breath, you go back and forth with low to high CO_2. Your body pH goes back and forth as well. This triggers your sympathetic nervous system, so you're ready for fight or flight. It prepares both my body and my state of mind, the desired state of mind in which I want to be when I conduct the mission because that memory will be the imprint for this mission in the future. Remember, don't prepare or plan in the wrong state of mind. You may bring negative emotion, such as fear, into the future.

> Create a state of mind that works for you and get into that state of mind before you start. Surgical, steely eyed, deliberate, and decisive—like a pilot in a storm—usually works well for high-stress tasks.

"Brace for Impact"

In 2009, US Airways pilot Captain Chesley Sullenberger (Sully) departed from LaGuardia airport in New York in the cockpit of Flight 1549. Shortly after takeoff, the aircraft ran through a flock of Canada geese and lost power in both engines. With no power, Sully had to make a split-second decision not to return to the airport. Instead, he landed in the middle of the Hudson River, safely, with no loss of life. Can you imagine having to make that decision, knowing that so many lives—in the airplane and possibly on the ground—were at stake?

Ric Elias, a front-row passenger who did a TED Talk about the landing, says that the three most unemotional words he has ever heard uttered were Sully saying, "Brace for impact." Captain Sully and his copilot were calm and matter-of-fact, just as they'd been countless times in the flight simulator. They went through their emergency procedures as they would check off a grocery list—with no emotion, just focus. This is precisely how they had trained, and when the moment presented itself, they didn't just rise to the occasion, their training kicked into high gear. Being able to perform under pressure is not genetic; it is something we can manufacture and put in place for ourselves. It just takes deliberate effort.

> **Performance under pressure requires training and deliberate effort—and the willingness to fall back on your training when the critical moment arrives.**

Entering the Structure

I visualize myself standing at the door of a building waiting for the explosion to breach the door. I say out loud to myself: "Breathe, breathe, breathe." I do this so that when the time comes, I will instinctively breathe deeply *without* thinking about it.

People often hold their breath during stressful and strenuous events, but this can be detrimental to performance. I use all of my senses: I imagine the feel of the weapon in my hand, the smell of gun oil, and the sound of me saying my trigger phrase *in my mind* before entering the structure: "HOOYAH, mother-f***er!" Having my real weapon in hand during mind training gives me the feel and the smells to help me condition my mind. The intent is to ensure that when I'm on the "X" all of my senses will trigger the positive state of mind I had during training.

I see myself going through the door and taking my field of fire. I vocalize to myself the important points of performance—"weapon up, down the wall, hands, hands,

hands"—so that when I encounter someone, I don't look at their faces, I look at their hands because the hands hold the weapons. This dialogue controls my focus. I see my body position, walking smoothly on the balls of my feet, like a stalking lion, so that my steps don't jar my barrel and throw off my shots as I'm moving, and so that I don't trip over objects on the floor. I can smell the explosives and feel the glass under my feet. I look for details like the hinges of a door to know how it opens. It's all a very positive experience in my mind's eye, and I'm breathing deeply, eyes closed, smiling with intensity. I tell myself to breathe deeply, and I actually breathe deeply during the simulation training to make it a habit.

My words are guiding my thoughts and visual images during the whole scenario, so maintaining positive control of focus and language is critical. I see hallways, windows, furniture, doors, door hinges, and unknown people—I talk myself through all of it. I reinforce the positive moves completed in my mind with: "That's it, keep it up, move fast, scan the room, breathe, breathe, breathe." I also go through contingencies, such as malfunction drills for my weapon, or if shots are fired, how to react. Just like when the Chief entered the building and was immediately shot, he kept fighting through it and never quit. I go through these scenarios, so when shots are being fired and it's loud, I don't slow down, I continue to bring my A game.

This can go on forever. I train, visualizing different buildings, different scenarios. I try to remember the layout of specific buildings I've been in and how to clear them in my mind, just like Natan Sharansky running through chess scenarios when he was in solitary confinement. I never practice losing.

Frequently, I listen to music when doing mind training. Music speaks to the soul and helps create the state of mind, so my choice of music varies, depending on the mission. My go-to for combat was AC/DC.

The key is knowing the exact points of performance for the mission, and bringing all your tools to bear on the training. If you do it properly, you can generate the alpha flow state. It's essential to visualize all the details, so when you do it for real, you get a sense of déjà vu. Familiarity will help inoculate you from fear.

TO THE LIONS? OR TO THE SIMULATOR?

These examples may seem extreme. After all, how many of you are planning to engage in CQB combat in your workplace? Here I'll try to bring this mind-training regimen home to a much-feared activity that plays out every day in the workplace: public speaking.

As you know, before I started speaking professionally, I was not used to being vulnerable on stage. I realized that the hardest part for me was to "be myself"; to actually speak on stage as if I was simply having a conversation with someone and expressing myself with authenticity. I had to learn to let my personality come out, and not be a stoic "steely-eyed" Navy SEAL. I had to connect with the audience and get rid of my doubts.

One of my main challenges was confidence in my message. Although, intellectually, I knew that my experiences have given me deep and profound lessons to pass on, if something is so familiar to you, it's easy to think that it's common knowledge and nothing special. But that was my fear talking, fear of being ridiculed for stating the obvious. I had to remind myself that what was obvious to me was not obvious to *them*, my audience—and that my intent was to inspire them to change, to touch them, to connect with them, and to bring them an aha moment that would become a seed growing within them.

Mind Preparation

I started constructing my state of mind, which is one of humility, service, and stewardship toward my audience. "Customer focus," you might say. It's not "look at me" time; it's a time for me to give everything I can give to the audience. I must be sure they want to hear what I have to say, and I need to be at my best to deliver it. After my first few professional speaking engagements following the publication of *First, Fast, Fearless*, I learned a lot about how I needed to prepare. What I discovered surprised me!

As a SEAL officer, I spoke to rooms of hundreds of people, but I had never spoken to so many people not paying attention! Even worse, some were talking to each other or playing on their phones. The first time this happened, I felt an enormous loss in confidence right there on stage—and when you've lost your confidence, 40 minutes on stage in front of a crowd is a lifetime. Anxiety and anger kicked in because I had never experienced this before; it was a surprise for which I hadn't planned. In the military, this conduct would simply not be tolerated. You would be reprimanded and possibly kicked out of the room. Paying attention is part of your job.

Developing the Habit

I had a lot of work to do in the simulator. It was critical for me to get better without having to go on stage to make mistakes and fumble around. The content and organization weren't the issues. I needed to work on my delivery. More important, I needed to work on my state of mind. I knew that people who often don't pay attention can be the ones who need to the most. I knew that no matter what happens in the crowd, I had to bring my best. And I also knew that deep down, they wanted to hear what I had to say.

I called the points of performance that I concentrated on for delivery VEGA (voice, eye contact, gestures, and attitude). I had to excite the audience. I needed to be the cause of the effect, not the effect that was caused! I wasn't there to mirror them; I needed them to mirror me. I don't feed off the crowd; they feed off me. We all know what it means to dance as if no one is watching. Now my goal is to speak this way, to let go and be present on stage.

PUTTING STATE-OF-MIND
TRAINING INTO PRACTICE

This process of training for a state of mind can be used for any aspect of our lives: interviewing for a job, making a presentation, giving a performance review to an employee, negotiating a promotion or raise, inviting someone on a date, having a difficult conversation, or improving at a sport. It's critical to have faith in the process, use the tools that you have, and practice perfect points of performance during the session in your mind. You must train with the state of mind you want to have during the event so that you are able to replicate it when the time comes.

Leave the Bad Stuff Behind

This process can even be done on past events. We can revisit them, learn from them, and change our perception of what the events meant and how we currently feel about them—an After Action Review (AAR) of sorts. Before I revisited my memories, I knew that I had to change my state of mind before I reexamined them, so I went for a run. I went back to the past, taking my present state of mind—happy with who I am and accountable for what happens in my life.

When I go back in time, I change my dialogue. I've even apologized and asked for forgiveness for things that cannot be changed. I revisit these memories with a positive state of mind. I don't want to carry my past fears and horrors into the future. What we often call "collateral damage" is not as sterile as it sounds from a distance. There is nothing "collateral" about it when you are up close to it; it is *damage*. But I choose not to be a victim in life, and I refuse to have negative feelings, memories, and incidents shape my future. I decide to be the cause of the effect, not the effect that was caused.

My deliberate effort to revisit my thoughts and memories in my simulator helped change how I felt about them. I was able to shift my feelings about the past to one of gratitude for all of the experiences that got me to where I am today. The feelings that come from the past are, in some sense, in our control. We can't change the event, but we can change how we feel about the event.

The simulator in our mind gives us a place to practice situations and responses in any aspect of our lives. The beauty of this training is that we are in control of how we train and ultimately, how we live.

Be the cause of the effect.

EXERCISE

Reflect on your life and identify what you wish to accomplish and the things that worry you. Establish a deliberate mental process using the principles in this chapter. Set your intentions, control your state of mind, and use first strike language to guide your visualization and see success. Repeat these visualizations as you move toward your goals.

TAKEAWAYS

- By controlling how we think and what we think, we control the destiny of our lives.

- Neuroscientists have found that the same neuron circuits fire in the brain when we *perform* an action and when we *imagine* performing the action.

- The mind is command center, practice simulator, and time machine—all in one.

- When training the mind, state your intent, prepare your body, keep positive, use first strike language, visualize, use your senses, and breathe.

- When revisiting negative aspects of the past, use a current positive mindset. Don't relive a past negative mindset. You'll bring the fear right into the present and then on into the future.

- The simulator in our mind gives us a place to practice situations and responses in any aspect of our lives.

- Be the cause of the effect. It's your choice.

10

LUCK BY DESIGN

Using Multipliers to Shape the Battlefield

A primary reason for the success of SEAL Teams is *preparation*. We are so prepared before the fight that our confidence is high, we feel optimistically lucky, and we are able to draw on GUTS.

Before a military invasion, it's imperative to prepare the battlefield in your favor and not leave it to chance. We call this *shaping the battlefield* or *preparing the battlefield*. Before invading or sending in conventional military forces, Special Forces conducts missions, such as reconnaissance, sabotage, spy development, deception, creating indigenous partner forces, disrupting communications, extracting VIPs, and more. We make the battlefield conducive for our success, not our enemy's. Life is no different; the more we prepare ourselves and shape our environments, the better our chance of success. It often appears to be luck—but it isn't.

> Every battle is won before it's ever fought.
>
> —SUN TZU

NAKED WARRIORS

Our SEAL forefathers, the Naked Warriors—so called because they went on missions wearing only swim trunks, fins, and masks—did nothing but shape operations in World War II. Days before every major beach landing, the Naked Warriors would swim onto the beaches bearing nothing but a knife and a bag of explosives to clear the beaches of obstacles. This was in preparation for the landing craft that would carry the Marines and soldiers who were to storm the beach. During the landing in Guam, the Naked Warriors performed continuous operations for six days, clearing more than 900 obstacles before the landings, and suffering nearly 75 percent casualties. Few people even knew they existed. These archetypal frogmen were the predecessors of all Navy SEALs. While our mission has evolved over the years, deep down, we SEALs all identify as frogmen who are willing to do what others can't or won't.

WHAT ARE MULTIPLIERS?

In your professional and personal lives, the way you shape your own battlefield—or environment—has a direct effect on you and your success. Your environment will evolve you, so why not shape your environment and facilitate your evolution?

Multipliers refer to the things we can do to exponentially increase our potential for success. The results produce a compounding effect, providing maximum outcomes for minimum effort and commitment. Multipliers are particularly important for transformational, or strategic, aspects of our lives, and deliver the greatest value.

The "Shape Charge" Effect

In the Special Forces, we perform small but transformational duties, such as preparing the battlefield or clearing the harbor, that have a significant strategic impact on the global mission. We don't fight wars the way conventional forces do, but, if correctly utilized, we do have a significant impact on the outcome. As of early 2020, Special Forces personnel are deployed in 149 different countries, supporting the internal defense of nations around the world. We embed small units of Special Forces members in other militaries to organize, man, train, equip, and ultimately lead them into battle or prepare them to defend their national interests. The effect these units have on global security is far greater than the sum of their small numbers. To put this into context, the United Nations only recognizes 195 countries; we cover more than three out of every four.

To explain this role, the SEAL Teams use the "shaped charge effect" metaphor; that is, SEALs create a "shaped charge effect" whenever we are involved in an operation. What is a shaped charge, you might ask? A shaped charge occurs when you put two or more explosive devices at the proper angle and distance from the surface of an object, so that when detonated, the explosives collide with each other and form a knifelike jet of energy that can cut through surfaces, increasing the impact of the explosives exponentially. In the movies, when you see a team blow off a heavy steel door, they are likely using a shaped charge approach. If this weren't used, the amount of explosives it would take to blow off a metal door would probably kill or render unconscious anyone nearby who set off the explosive. For instance, if you place 40 pounds of explosives on the ground and detonate them, you may end up with a tapered hole four feet in diameter with a center one foot deep, as most of the energy blows up and out, not down. But if you take that same amount of explosive and shape it properly, you could get a 10-foot-deep hole that is one foot in diameter, depending on the soil makeup. The shape charge effect is a force multiplier. It gives us the most bang for the buck—literally!—exponentially increasing the odds for success. SEALs use the shaped charge effect in their operations and act as a shaped charge themselves in their missions.

Humor and Play

People are at their best during play. Anyone who is around SEALs for long will quickly learn about our culture of play and humor. It may be a coping mechanism for the dangers of the profession, or it may just have to do with the type of people we recruit and train. Either way, the effect of play and humor cannot be ignored in our success. Even during our most serious missions, when the tension can be cut with a knife, we use humor to cut it instead. When you can laugh and have fun in the face of death, you're not only living in the moment, you're increasing your odds of success. Remember, the executive parts of our brain shut down when we're in a fearful state of mind; since we can't have two states of mind at the same time, we focus on play in the moment instead of worrying about the future. Humor keeps your mind nimble, focused, and flexible, and it enables you to access your best creative self during the darkest and worst of times. A playful state of mind helps change your perception of the events happening around you. You even get a DOSE and reduce cortisol. Good leaders use self-deprecation, making everyone around them more comfortable and creating a better environment for the team to thrive.

> Life is a one-way dead-end street; it's too serious to take too seriously.

Some of the scariest times have ultimately turned into some of the funniest moments in my life. I remember one night, as my unit was driving in Iraq on a mission, one of the vehicles in our convoy was hit by an improvised explosive device (IED). It detonated just before the vehicle drove over it. Had the explosion happened milliseconds later, the vehicle would have been destroyed, and most likely, everyone inside would have been killed or wounded. Luckily, nobody was seriously hurt.

After the mission, we ensured everyone was OK and we conducted an After Action Review (AAR). "Country Dave," the turret gunner hit by the IED, started to explain what had happened. He was full of emotion and was very animated in his storytelling. He was yelling very loudly because, as you can imagine, the explosion had done a number on his hearing. We realized he couldn't hear worth a damn. All at once it seemed, we all busted out laughing hysterically, the type of laughter that only comes after a seriously tense situation is resolved. Dave was a little mad that we were laughing at him, but the scene was one right out of a cartoon. His face was solid black, just like a cartoon character who, holding a bowling ball bomb, has it go off in his face, covering him in soot. Although the blast nearly killed him, we almost died laughing, and then, so did he.

I still remember him saying in his "Country Dave" voice, "It ain't f***ing funny. I 'bout got blowed up, and y'all are laughing like it's funny, like a bunch of damn fools!" But eventually, the laughter caught on, and Dave started laughing hysterically at himself after realizing he was yelling with a face as black as night.

Some people might think such laughter is sick and thoughtless, but no, it's a weapon against suffering, despair, and fear. Laughter in the face of possible traumatic events and life challenges is a way to give the middle finger to the grim reaper, As Friedrich Nietzsche said, "That which does not kill us makes us stronger." In this case, laughing in the face of adversity creates and celebrates a sense of optimism, luck, and esprit de corps; it makes us stronger. If we sat around dwelling and awfulizing about what could have happened, you can bet it would have cemented this event in our minds as something horrific. But laughter gives us a DOSE, changing the way we perceive the event, and, more importantly, how we carry that memory forward.

> **That which does not kill us**
> **makes us stronger.**
> **—FRIEDRICH NIETZSCHE**

Rituals

I have a routine I follow religiously before every mission. How I put my gear on, in what order, and even the mental process of getting ready are part of this routine. Developed in my initial training, I do it the same way every single time, no matter what. This ritual provides familiarity and comfort in the things I know and have done countless times; it helps prepare me mentally for the fight. It's also a great way to develop a checklist and to make sure that, in times of stress, I don't forget something important.

One night in Iraq, I was leading a force of American soldiers to create a perimeter around a target compound for a direct action mission to be carried out by my Task Force. The target building was in Sadr City, a dangerous place, and everyone on the mission knew it. We all knew it wasn't a matter of *if* we would encounter the enemy; it was a matter of *when*. Before departure, a young Army soldier climbed into the back seat, beside me. We were about to leave the walled compound when I noticed that the soldier didn't have his rifle. I leaned over to him, and said something to the effect of "Hey bro, go back and get your gun. You might need it." Holy moly, he almost had a panic attack! He jumped out of the vehicle, ran back to the staging area, and got his weapon. Of course, when he returned, I laughed at him and told him he owed me a case of beer (which I, of course, never received). He didn't have a ritual, and due to his fear, forgot a critical step in preparing for the mission—his *gun*!

Rituals build discipline. Design and create rituals that you enjoy and look forward to, so that they become repeatable habits. Good habits are like a checklist to help ensure important steps are taken. Over time they define who you are, what you do, and how you do it. I am very proactive in creating rituals around what I want to improve in my life.

Beginning with Gratitude

Early morning is my favorite time of day. I start my day by being grateful that I'm alive and thankful for the day. I challenged myself to begin this daybreak ritual as soon as I could remember to do it. At first, I would forget occasionally; it would take me as long as 20 minutes after waking to remember to be grateful. But it didn't take me long to get to the point where I remembered it immediately upon waking, even before I came out of the haze between consciousness and sleep.

I now spend several minutes after waking, filling my reticular activating system (RAS) with gratitude for all that I have in my life—not just the big things like health, family, friends, money, and shelter, but even the small things we usually don't think of, such as running water, electricity, security, and technology.

Practicing gratitude for having whatever job you have will help you strengthen your relationship with it and manufacture motivation. If, when you wake up, you automatically go into a dreadful state of mind, it will affect your whole day negatively. This special time of lying in bed, intentionally feeling grateful, is the key to starting the day with a state of mind that will act as a positive filter and compass to guide you.

When we practice gratitude for what we have in our lives, we build a better relationship with those things. I challenge everyone to try this and keep note of how long it takes to remember to do it in the morning. Once it happens immediately, then you've built a habit, one that enables your subconscious mind to point you in a good direction.

> **Early morning gratitude—intentionally feeling grateful—is the key to starting each day with a positive state of mind.**

When I get up early, I'm already excited about being awake. I start the coffee, pour myself a quart of cold sparkling water mixed with a little lemon juice, and sit on the couch to begin my breathing techniques. I hyperventilate for at least 30 breaths, blow out all the air, and hold my breath for as long as possible. Then I inhale and hold this for 10 seconds. I do this three times, which gets my sympathetic nervous system up and running. I exercise with low impact movements, all while breathing through my stomach and practicing gratitude and/or visualizing what I'm about to do to create a positive state of mind.

After 15 minutes of this, I take my coffee and water and sit in front of the computer. I look at my notes from the day before, so I know where to begin. Often, I watch a funny video or read something exciting and positive that's related to what I am doing that day. I have sticky notes with quotes and thoughts all over my desk, which force me to fill my RAS with what I want. Mornings are my most productive time of day, when my brain is working well, and I'm focused, excited, and just grateful to be alive. By the time I've had two cups of coffee and at least two quarts of water, and have worked for several hours, I go for a workout. If I'm on a roll, I wait; sometimes it's near noon, but no matter what, I get my exercise in. During this workout/therapy session, I've discovered that if I'm stuck on something, I often have it figured out by the time I get back to my desk. Moving the body allows time for our minds to put patterns together and gain insights into our lives.

Luck

Luck is important, but the type of luck I am referring to is not about winning the lottery or being struck by lightning. Rather, the "luck" involved here is the type that we can manufacture and control. In the world of work, and in our personal lives to some degree, we can multiply force by putting ourselves in position to achieve a favorable outcome. For example, a favorable geographic location for a store increases its chances for success. A favorable business presentation starts with choosing a venue in which you feel most comfortable, and eliminating potential distractions and disrupters, such as noise. Being prepared and being likeable might give you an opportunity to deliver an elevator pitch at an opportune moment that can change your life. When disciplined preparation meets opportunity, it often appears to be luck, but is it? In this sense, you "manage the randomness" of the situation to tilt toward a favorable outcome, something we do all the time in the SEAL world.

Every SEAL I know feels lucky. We feel that, no matter what, we will win in the end. Even if the odds are not good, we have a great deal of optimism about the outcome. And when something terrible happens, SEALs immediately think that it could have been worse, so by default, we are grateful for the event because it probably taught us something.

Feeling lucky is a sign of what goes on in your mind—if you are optimistic and can control your focus, language, thoughts, and emotions—you're predisposed to having things work out right. I've found that the best way to hack the feeling of being lucky is to practice gratitude in all aspects of life. Gratitude creates a positive and optimistic state of mind, which leads to a lucky state of mind. If you focus on gratitude, you will always feel lucky.

ONE AND ONE IS THREE: SWIM BUDDIES

When *First, Fast, Fearless* came out, I had people from all industries contacting me for speaking engagements and leadership training. One topic that really resonated was the SEAL concept of swim buddies. People reached out to me and told me they were implementing this concept in their organizations. One senior leader in particular, Jeremey Donovan, not only said he was implementing this across his entire company, but he also recommended this be my topic for a TED Talk, which meant a lot because he is the author of the book *How to Deliver a TED Talk*.

From the very beginning of training to the time we leave the SEAL Teams or retire, each SEAL must have a person with him, no matter what he is doing. We start applying this requirement in BUD/S. Up and down the beach all day, you will hear students yelling: "Swim buddy, I need a swim buddy!" This is one of the disciplined habits we instill in our students to prepare them for the VUCA (volatility, uncertainty, complexity, and ambiguity) of war. We don't know what the students will face when they get to the SEAL Teams, but we do know that they will encounter VUCA and have to deal with very fearsome, dangerous, and complicated situations. We know that being with another person makes us stronger, braver, smarter, and more capable of solving complex problems; it brings our focus into the now. Humans are social beings. This is why, under the Geneva Convention, which established the standards of international law for humanitarian treatment in war, isolation for extended periods of time is considered a form of torture. During the Covid-19 pandemic many people suffered mental distress and depression because of the forced isolation and physical distancing that kept people—even family members—apart.

> Find a swim buddy. We know that being
> with another person makes us stronger,
> braver, smarter, and more capable of solving
> complex problems; it brings our
> focus into the now.

Joint Accountability

The foundation of all teamwork starts with the swim buddy team of two people. Accountability is shared and overlapping, meaning each member of the pair is held 100 percent accountable for the mission as if it was theirs alone. Most people would say that each person should be 50 percent accountable, but by doing that, you open the door to excuses and a path to failure. Once a swim pair realizes it doesn't matter who does what because they both are 100 percent owners of the mission, it eliminates the seams and gaps that may occur when each person is only 50 percent accountable. Once embraced, this overlapping accountability creates a shape charge effect, and the whole becomes much greater than the sum of its parts. The swim buddy system eliminates the "I, me, and mine" language, unless one of the members is taking responsibility for a failure.

In Sight Gets It Right

The Observation Effect holds that the act of observing something will influence that which is being observed. In quantum mechanics, through the double-slit experiment, scientists have found that observation, even passive observation, will change the behavior at the photon level. In psychology, the Hawthorne Effect occurs when subjects modify their behavior when they know they are being observed. One study, called the "Princess Alice" experiment, had some young children playing a simple game with easy rules. The kids, observed by a hidden camera, cheated when they were alone. When the scientist tested another group of kids, they were told that "Princess Alice" sat invisibly on an empty chair in the room. As you might guess, the kids followed the rules as long as they believed Princess Alice was watching. The power of the Observation Effect has been around for all of recorded history, mostly in our experience of religion and its invisible gods. If you believe that God is watching you, does that lead to better behavior?

Of course, we all know that there are things we do in private that we don't do in the company of another person. I consider myself one of the best dancers and singers on this planet—at least when I am by myself!

Studies have shown that simply putting a picture of a set of eyes over the money jar in the office will significantly increase the amount of money employees will leave in the "honor jar." Having a swim buddy with eyes on you will help you stay accountable.

The Power of "Others Focus"

The swim buddy system, with overlapping fields of accountability, also creates a sense of "others focus." When we focus on others, we get a DOSE and form strong bonds, which help to mitigate fear and doubt. During the toughest times, we want our teammates not to focus on themselves, but rather on others. This takes them away from the awfulizing and isolation that destroys courage and confidence and increases the chance of failure. We are more productive, and the memories of events are stronger when we share them with someone else.

The swim buddy concept is one of the easiest and most straightforward SEAL operating concepts to implement in your professional and personal life. Hell, I'm working with a swim buddy right now to write this book!

> **When in doubt, find a swim buddy.**
> **One plus one is three!**

ALWAYS PLAY FOR
YOUR REPUTATION

As SEALs, we take our reputations very seriously. You may not know your reputation, but you can bet the people around you do! We have a saying in the SEAL Teams, "A thousand attaboys don't make up for one 'Oh f***!'" Our brains are designed to see danger, focus on threats, and pick up on the negative, so if we do something wrong, that's often what people remember. Learn to apologize, stay on high moral ground, and always play for your reputation.

You reap what you sow. Whatever you put out into the world, you will find yourselves receiving down the road. Do what will make you more respected, more trustworthy, and more likable, and you will have a greater influence in the world. Attract good people into your life.

Ask yourself: "Do you deserve, and do you generate envy?" When your reputation is strong, and you're doing things right, people will envy you.

Your reputation is like a shadow that beats you to the party and stays in the room long after you're gone.

TRUST

In the SEAL Teams, we lay it out pretty simply: "If we can't trust you, we cannot use you." We don't care how good of a performer someone is, if he is not trustworthy, we do not want him in our organization. People who cannot be trusted will tear an organization apart. We have had gifted SEALs—SEALs who were amazing athletes, great problem solvers, and very capable—but we kicked them out for lack of trust. We would take someone with medium performance and high trust over someone with high performance and medium trust every time. Trust is earned. It's not given freely nor should it be, so go on the offensive and earn it. I have a simple five-point TRUST model that I use for building trust in a team or in life.

Time and Attention

Say what you're going to do, and do what you say. Do what you say *when* you say you're going to do it. Time is finite, and we all must pay attention to how we choose to spend it. When you waste someone's time, he or she loses a commodity that cannot be gotten back; everyone resents it. I hear it in the corporate world, "The boss is never late. The meeting time is when she gets there." This is often said in a joking manner, but in reality, it's not a sign of good leadership, and people know it.

You have to view your time and attention (focus), which equals effort, as valuable commodities, just like money. Since writing *First, Fast, Fearless*, I've done a lot of free coaching, speaking, and even consulting, and I have found that most people don't value time unless you put a price on it. It's not uncommon for someone that I've done free coaching or consulting for to show up late or to not even show up! But when I charge for my services, the person shows up ready to squeeze every drop out of me and demanding my full attention. Time and attention are valuable. Don't waste yours, and respect and appreciate that of others.

> **Say what you're going to do, and do what you say.**
>
> **Do what you say *when* you say you're going to do it.**

Respect

Every human being wants to be respected. Our lives are valuable to us, and we want to feel they are valuable to others as well. Respect is a way of reinforcing that. You can learn a lot about people by how they treat others. Do they respect the janitor the same way they respect the CEO? When they feel powerful, do they abuse that power? Do they do a great job of leading up, but a poor one of leading down? When we disrespect people, especially in public, they do not forget it easily, nor should they. When we disrespect people, we are telling them that we do not consider them as our equal. If we truly value life, then we realize that every life is equal. As evangelical author Rick Warren wrote in his book *The Purpose-Driven Life*, "Humility is not thinking less of yourself, but thinking of yourself less." We need to practice humility, not humiliation.

> **Humility is not thinking less of yourself,**
>
> **but thinking of yourself less.**
>
> **—RICK WARREN**

Unbreakable Values

Our actions, over time, represent our beliefs and our values. Every day, we have to prioritize our values to navigate the world and the way we see ourselves in it. I believe the number one value we should all have is life itself. I believe courage is right up there with life as a value because if we don't have courage, we can't exercise the values we believe in.

Our natural default mode is to believe people when they say something, but be mindful. Pay attention to what people *do* more than what they say, and you'll discover who they really are. People will know your values based on your behavior, so let your values lead your actions.

Sacrifice

Do you give more than you take, in relationships, at work, and in life in general? Do you produce more than you consume? The foundation of any team is trust, and the secret sauce of trust is the willingness to sacrifice for the mission and for others, to delay personal gratification, and in extreme situations, to delay even your own safety.

We have a technique to teach sacrifice to young officers: for mealtime, we instruct them to go to the back of the line. Officers do not eat until after the enlisted people have eaten. As we say, "The higher you go, the more you owe." It's not about privilege; it's about giving. We all know the people who give more than they take—not only do we want them on our team, we want them *leading* our team.

Technical Proficiency

As I said earlier, "It takes a shooter to lead a shooter." That goes for all aspects of life. If we are on a team, and we don't know our job and we aren't progressing and evolving, it's hard for the team to trust us. Our SEAL Ethos says, "My training is never complete." We must continue to learn and grow. Always.

> **Trust is a peek behind the curtain of our character.**

PASSING DOWN THE CULTURE: SEA STORIES

Since it was first established in 1775, it's been a Navy tradition to come back from sea and tell "sea stories"—stories of adventure and hardship, exotic ports, and the allure of life at sea. The Navy has boot camp and Officer Candidate School, but those aren't nearly as effective at passing down the culture to new sailors as these sea stories, and each generation takes pride in telling their own. Sea stories are compelling and influence the behaviors and beliefs of new sailors more than any of the organized programs through which the Navy formally puts recruits. For good or bad, the sea stories we tell influence others, build our own reputation, and embed organizational culture.

In 2005, after several years of multiple wars, the SEAL Teams realized that we had a cultural divide in our own perception of what a Navy SEAL really was and wasn't. When we developed our ethos to govern our behavior on and off the battlefield, we knew the place to start was not just in the classroom but on the beaches and ranges of BUD/S training during the downtime between the curriculum and training evolutions. We had to communicate our ethos clearly through our sea stories. If our sea stories didn't match our stated way of life, our ethos would be nothing but a piece of paper visited a couple of times a year.

When Culture and Values Don't Match

The stories we tell at work and in our personal lives are an expression of our values and beliefs. People learn a lot about you through the stories you tell. I did some work for a large power company that wanted my help getting through to their frontline managers about safety. Parts of their business were very dangerous, and, like the SEAL Teams, they had a culture that they wanted to modify, or at least define, so that they could move forward in the direction they wanted. Although this company had done great work in developing and enforcing a thorough safety program, they still had mishaps that could easily have been prevented. In a dangerous profession, it's very easy to develop a macho cowboy mindset due to the nature of the job and the people you recruit.

At the hotel bar the night before the event, it didn't take long for me to identify a problem not being addressed— they had not changed their frontline sea stories. The foremen who had been around for a long time loved telling stories to the younger workers about how, when they were young, they did stupid things and broke the rules, yet lived through it.

Of course, they would qualify their stories by saying, "But now we are smarter than that. That stuff is no longer tolerated. And, boy, are we lucky to be alive." Those stories completely contradicted the company's safety policies, but they had the allure of danger, which appealed to the young workers, who wanted to tell their own exciting sea stories to a younger generation one day. Let's face it, it's hard to start off a "good story" with: "There I was following every safety procedure, and lo and behold, the job went off without a glitch, and we all went home to our families."

Once the president of the company learned this concept, he immediately recognized the problem. He vowed to start teaching the frontline foremen about the powerful influence their stories have on new workers and company safety.

The stories we tell are windows into our character, our values, and our beliefs. Do we tell stories in which we are always the victim, always being wronged, or blaming others for what happens to us? Or do we tell stories of humility, accountability, kindness, and fairness? What are the common themes in our stories? How we weave our values into our stories is important in shaping our world. Our stories are a leadership tool that can shape not only our teams and culture, but the very battlefield of life.

You can build your reputation by being intentional about your stories and how you recall events so that they represent who you are and who you want to be. Your stories have to tell the truth about who you are. In the same way, sea stories have to be aligned with a company's culture and values.

Courageous Restraint

Communication expert Julian Treasure identified the seven deadly sins of speaking: gossiping, judging, negativity, complaining, excuses, exaggeration, and dogmatism. All are fear based, and to stop them, it takes an essential form of courage, a kind of courage called *courageous restraint*. Being able to restrain ourselves is just as crucial as delaying gratification. It takes the "emotions off our sleeves" and shows others that we, in fact, are in control of them.

In 2010, I was in Afghanistan working with Afghan Special Forces when a new concept came out of the headquarters that struck me as interesting. The United States was considering establishing a medal for "courageous restraint" for military personnel who showed physical restraint on the battlefield. The mantra at the time in Iraq and Afghanistan stated that we could not "kill our way to victory." When you're trying to win the hearts and minds of a country in an insurgency, it's a delicate balance to maintain the safety of friendly troops and to control the escalation of violence. Sadly, the idea of the medal was shot down quickly.

The military awards medals for valor and courage, which usually means gunfights resulting in the deaths of enemies. As much as we preach about not killing our way to victory, the number of Direct Action missions and enemies killed are high on our After Action Reviews (AARs) and on our personal evaluations. You get what you reward.

Military people may say they don't care about medals, but I've found the reverse to be true. Such recognition drives behavior and sea stories, which then drives culture. You don't hear sea stories about courageous restraint. You hear stories of extreme physical courage and heroic gunfights. Just as with the large power company, the stories encouraged certain behaviors.

Some of the bravest and most decent acts I witnessed in combat were of SEALs practicing courageous restraint when no one would have questioned their use of violence. Courageous restraint is a heroic virtue to which we should all aspire. Do we have the courage not to get the last word, not to be passive-aggressive, not to blame others, not to commit the seven deadly sins of communicating? Your reputation is created by what you show, tell, and do. Having restraint will help you build your reputation, and will allow you to refrain from what I call "picking fights with the devil"—getting into lose-lose situations. The best position in every professional and personal relationship we have is a win-win position. Courageous restraint will help your relationships become win-win and will ultimately produce "luck" for you, the kind of luck you create by doing the right thing.

Learn to Listen and You Learn a Lot

I can't talk about sea stories without talking about listening. Listening is an art and takes deliberate intent, empathy, and the right state of mind. I once asked leadership expert and bestselling author Ken Blanchard, my good friend and mentor, why he chooses to coauthor books instead of writing them alone. His response was perfect: "I already know what I know, so why would I write by myself?" It is also no surprise that Ken is one of the best listeners I've ever been around.

Most of our time in conversations is spent waiting to respond. Our minds are formulating our next conversational move, and we don't truly feel and hear the other person speaking. I'm no different. As an executive coach, I'll admit that it took me a while to learn to listen, or at least listen deeply. Focusing on what the client was saying and silencing the blabbermouth in my mind was tough at first. I wanted to speak and contribute to the conversation, like we all do. Just like learning to focus during meditation, *focus listening* is a muscle we must train.

> **Focus listening is a muscle we must train.**

Before the executive coaching sessions, I had to get in an empathetic state of mind, so that I could direct my focus on the client and listen deeply. The client would tell sea stories of his lives, how things were going at work and how things were going at home. When I focused on the client, I could really hear his intent, his problems due to fear. This may sound like I'm stating the obvious, but we can learn a lot as disciplined listeners. To see if I was hearing what a client was saying, I would paraphrase what I heard back to him. Often, he would disagree and go into more detail. I would repeat this exercise until the client agreed with my description of his situation. By practicing courageous restraint in conversation, I also learned that people just want someone to listen to them, someone to hold them accountable—just like a good swim buddy. It is only by being intentional about listening that you learn. As the great Ken Blanchard said, you already know what you know.

The words we use are only a small part of communicating. Our voice and our body language are better indications of what we mean than the words we use, so remember to pay attention to the whole person. Find the intent behind what is said.

EXERCISE

Your reputation is a shadow of your character, so be deliberate about building it with sea stories that reflect your values and beliefs. Identify your three top values or beliefs. Reflect on your life and choose a story you can tell for each value. Craft the story intentionally so it clearly communicates to others exactly who you are.

TAKEAWAYS

- It's imperative to prepare the battlefield in your favor and not leave it to chance. SEALs call this *shaping the battlefield* or *preparing the battlefield*.

- The more we prepare ourselves and shape our environment, the better chance we have at success. This often appears to be luck.

- Multipliers increase our potential for success exponentially.

- The "shape charge" effect is a force multiplier. SEALs use the shaped charge effect in many operations, and they act as a shaped charge themselves in their missions.

- Humor and play as force multipliers will help keep your mind nimble, focused, and flexible. They allow you to access your best creative self.

- Rituals, another force multiplier, should be something you enjoy and look forward to so that they become positive, repeatable habits. Rituals build discipline.

- The swim buddy concept is one of the easiest and most straightforward SEAL operating concepts to implement in your professional and personal lives. One plus one equals three.

- Our reputation is like a shadow that beats us to the party and stays in the room long after we're gone.

- Trust is earned. It's not given freely nor should it be, so go on the offensive and earn it.

- Humility is not thinking less of yourself, but thinking of yourself less.

- The sea stories we tell are windows into our character, our values, and our beliefs. They are a leadership tool that can shape not only our teams and culture but the very battlefield of life.

- Courageous restraint is a heroic virtue to which we should all aspire.

11

PLANNING

Fail to Plan, Plan to Fail

The old adage "No plan survives the first contact with the enemy" or the better known Mike Tyson corollary "No plan survives past the first punch" are a bit off the mark. They tend to give the impression that operating as an ad hoc cowboy, adapting and adjusting everything as we go, is the way of the elite; that's a little misleading. Another popular expression "Those that fail to plan, plan to fail" is actually more accurate. For everything we do on the SEAL Teams, there is a plan, a brief, and rehearsals before executing the evolution or mission.

Developing such plans is crucial to reducing anxiety and fear. In combat, if you lose focus and default to daydreaming and awfulizing, you may wind up in a state of extreme debilitating fear. Planning and preparation decrease fear by keeping you in the present rather than awfulizing about the future.

Planning is actually taking action, and taking action gives you confidence in your success and addresses the fearful unknowns. SEALs come up with detailed plans so that on a mission, when we are cold, wet, tired, scared, and something goes wrong, we know what to do. When the pressure is highest and our executive brains are shut down, we don't rely on innovation—we fall back on our plan.

Our mission planning, operations planning, and decision-making planning processes could fill many books. I will condense it down to the processes we use that will best fit the needs in your personal and professional lives.

> **The time to repair the roof is**
> **when the sun is shining.**
> **—JOHN F. KENNEDY**

THE FIGHT TRIANGLE

We have three main elements that come into play for every mission, every operation, everything we do; I call it the *fight triangle*. The triangle consists of surprise, speed, and violence of action. Whether you are assaulting a target or planning a project, these three elements, taken together, are essential to success. In the SEAL world, if we lose one of these elements during a mission, the danger increases and our probability of success reduces.

The Element of Surprise

It's not hard to understand that the best time to attack is when the enemy doesn't expect it; you catch them by surprise before they can prepare or react. Some of the best missions I've led were ones in which the enemy had no idea we were coming. Often, we would catch them asleep; sometimes they didn't wake up until we were standing over them in their beds. The element of surprise is about taking the initiative and going on the offensive.

In BUD/S there is a concept I call the "leadership effect." Although the students are in the best shape of their lives, the instructors can beat them badly at most events just by taking the initiative.

Here's what I mean. During the rucksack marches, on which we carried 45-pound packs for 12 miles, mostly at a run, I used to crush the students, even though they were in their prime. They had to stay within a few feet behind me and could neither pass me nor fall behind. If they did, they would find themselves in a remediation session. I controlled the pace, and they had to forfeit their control to me. The group produced a "slinky effect": when I sped up without warning, the group spread out. They had no idea how much fuel I had in my tank or how long I could maintain the speed. They just had to endure in the unknown, which took away their ability to build a strategy. The back of the slinky had it worse because the adjustments were more pronounced.

Owning the element of surprise—the *initiative*—gave me "superhuman" strength versus the students who had no control over the situation. Taking the initiative gives you control, puts you on the offensive, and puts everyone else on the defensive. They must respond to you, not the other way around. In any organization, especially one characterized by a lack of communication, the further away from the decisions you are, the more at the back of the slinky you are. You feel less control, more jerked around, and less able to plan. I think most of us can relate to how decisions at the top jerk people at the bottom around. Whenever you can, take the initiative!

Speed Is of the Essence

While assaulting a target it's crucial to move with speed so that the opponent doesn't have time to regroup and adjust. In the corporate world, time is not your friend either. The imperative for change can be crushing. If something is critical or essential, it's important *now*!

Speed is important, and it has led, surprisingly, to one of the more important decisions I make at the beginning of certain missions: what size pack do I take? If I take too big a pack, I will fill it up, and it will slow me down. If I take too small a pack, I'll carry less and travel faster, but the saying "Go light; freeze at night" rattles through my head. This phrase, and others like it, helps us to prioritize correctly and take only what's essential for the mission.

It's easy to fill our professional and personal lives with things that aren't important, but if we want to create a sense of urgency to go faster and build momentum, we must take less time to do what needs to be done. Parkinson's Law states that "work expands to fill the time available for its completion." With this in mind, you can force yourself to create speed and momentum by restricting the time allowed to complete a task. This sense of urgency is contagious and creates followers around you.

First, Fast, and Forceful: Violence of Action

When the use of force becomes necessary, it's best to give it everything you have to overwhelm the enemy, so they have no opportunity to maneuver, adjust, or even figure out what's going on. This momentum in any attack is priceless; it can and will decide the outcome. Bold and overwhelming action is critical.

If you have watched a Mixed Martial Arts (MMA) fight, you'll notice that it's very different from conventional boxing. In boxing, if you knock down your opponent, you must wait 10 seconds to resume the attack, giving the opponent time to recover and regroup. In MMA if a fighter is knocked down, the other fighter jumps on his downed opponent immediately, overwhelming him with punches and violence of action. It's not uncommon for the underdog to win an MMA fight because, with the use of violence of action, the "better" fighter never gets an opportunity to regroup and adjust.

In work and life, attack a project with full force. Immerse yourself, commit, obsess—and *do*! Momentum is difficult to create, but when you gain it, you must maintain it. Like a flywheel, once it gets moving, it's hard to stop. Planning, discussing, and everything else we do to prepare are great, but a bias for action and violence of action, where appropriate, are necessary for success.

FIGURING OUT WHAT TO DO FIRST: MANAGING PRIORITIES

Our time, attention, and efforts are finite. We only have 24 hours in a day, so to achieve our goals and potential in life, we must prioritize. If we don't, it will be done for us by default. To make prioritization simple, I use three categories: "transformational," "transactional," and "*F*** that!*"

Transformational Priorities: Strategic Key Results

Transformational priorities are items that have a strategic impact on our success, accomplish the mission we seek to achieve, or transform our lives. In keeping with the Pareto principle of 80/20, we should spend 80 percent of our time doing these transformational activities.

I have a simple daily habit: at the end of the day I write down five things that I will do the following day, *no matter what* comes up. Unless something major happens—an emergency for instance—I will do those five things. The act of writing down a task or a goal has been proven over many studies to increase the likelihood of us accomplishing it. Some studies show that we are twice as likely to achieve what we write down.

I always put little boxes beside the items on my to-do list so that when I'm done with that task, I check it off and get a DOSE. I love seeing those boxes checked off!

> **Transform in the morning; transact at night.**

Transactional Priorities: Necessary but Not Strategic

Transactional items, such as filing documents to tidy up the office or cleaning the house, need to be done but don't transform our lives. These things matter, but our primary mission and goals in life will move forward without them. My goal is to spend only 20 percent of my time on these items. Usually I do transactional tasks only after I've completed some transformational priorities.

For example, I get up early and use that precious time to write because it is when my brain is working at its best. After my mind is tired, I go work out. Then I go through my transactional list and do at least one thing that doesn't require much brainpower but needs doing. At work, it's easy to find ourselves swamped with transactional items: answering emails, having meetings, browsing the internet, and more. It's easy to allow our time and attention to be stolen or dictated to us by someone or something else. It takes deliberate and offensive action to maintain control of our time, so make it a priority to do the tasks that will transform you and get you where you want to go.

> It takes deliberate and offensive action to maintain control of our time.

The "F***-That" List

In Chapter 1 I wrote about creating a "f***-it" list—a list of things you would do in life if it weren't for fear. Well, now it's time to create a "f***-*that*" list—a list of items that you will *not* prioritize, things that you don't care at all about but that you still may end up doing! If you're like me, then you know how easy it is to kill or waste time and not even know where it went. We do things that have no significant and positive impact on the outcome. Examples include going on social media, checking your phone, web surfing, unstructured daydreaming (worrying and awfulizing), watching TV, playing video games, texting relentlessly, picking fights with the devil, and spending time with negative people. I'm sure you can make a very comprehensive list. The key is to make that list, and literally, look at every item on that list and say, "F*** that!"

Knowing what to cut out will help you understand what's important. Furthermore, just by writing these lists, you will learn how you spend your time. Stop doing the worthless things that bring no value to your life, and you will find more time for the tasks that will improve your success.

When you take a moment to analyze what you do day in, day out, pay attention to how much of your time is *not* invested in critical transformation, and is either spent on transactional or "f*** that" items. The next step is to take each of your three lists and rank each item on it, from number one to the last. We know that if everything is important, then nothing is important, so as unpleasant as it is to have to put things at the bottom, it's important to show yourself what is and is not important. Remember, our time and attention are finite, so we must be intentional about how we spend them.

> **Our time and attention are finite, so we must be intentional about how we spend them.**

SEALS THE DEAL: A PLANNING FRAMEWORK

Like the corporate world, the SEAL world runs on acronyms; it seems like we have an acronym, catchphrase, or saying for everything. Planning is no different. What follows is my own personal five-point SEALS (specific, evaluable, actionable and attainable, leverageable, and scary) model for creating an actionable plan.

Specific

Earlier in the book, I talked about how critical it is to understand the situation and to know where you are, so you can identify and get where you want to go. If I'm lost in the woods and don't know where I am, I will have a harder time getting to where I want to go. It's often hard to be honest with ourselves; it's much easier to ignore the big elephant in our lives. We must learn to be brutally honest with ourselves without judgment. For example, if I want to lose a certain amount of body fat, I have to be honest about my starting point: my current body fat percentage, what foods I eat, how much I consume, how much I exercise, and the condition of my environment.

For every mission or goal, we have to answer the 5Ws (who, what, when, where, and why) to be specific. It's pretty straightforward, except sometimes we forget the power of our "why." "Why" is a significant motivator, so this question should be answered to understand the root of the task, the reason that will drive us over time when motivation is sparse.

> **What gets measured gets managed.**
>
> **—PETER DRUCKER**

Evaluable

If we can't measure something, how can we know we are progressing toward the goal, and how do we know when we get there? Some goals are simple: I want to lose 12 pounds in six months to fit into the dress uniform that I will wear to my best friend's wedding. I can measure this: every week or month, I can get on my scale and see what progress, if any, I've made. If I haven't made progress, I can adjust my habits to get on track.

I know if I lose two pounds a month for six months, I'll make my goal.

Some goals appear not to be measurable. For example, how do we measure happiness? We can do this by breaking it down into more easily measured goals. We know what make us happier: relationships, achieving goals, nature, exercise, nutrition, among other things. These can be measured. We know that spending time with a loved one makes us happy, so we can measure the amount of time we spend doing this and the number of people we do it with. We know that if we get a certain amount of exercise per day, then it makes us happy. When you decide to set a "soft" or abstract goal, make it as tangible as possible so that you can measure it and see progress. Progress is a fundamental ingredient to being happy. It gives us a DOSE!

> **What can be measured can be understood,**
> **what can be understood can be altered.**
> —KATHERINE NEVILLE, *THE EIGHT*

Actionable and Attainable

For every mission, we create an actionable plan. We start by reverse-engineering the mission, beginning with the actions at the objective, or the "X," and work our way backward to get there, going from X to A. Often, our missions are very complex, requiring us to coordinate with submarines, aircraft, indigenous forces, and other logistically challenging platforms. When planning we also have to answer the twin questions, "Is it attainable?" and "Are we prepared to accomplish the mission?"

We must be careful here. Often, we underestimate or overestimate our own abilities. The Pygmalion effect holds that the expectations others have of us influence our performance, so we need to go on the offensive and set high performance standards for ourselves. That in turn will influence others' expectations of us, and ultimately affect our beliefs toward ourselves. It's a positive circle. It's very similar to the *anchoring* effect that happens in negotiations in which the start price often dictates the end price because it anchors the initial price as a reference point. For instance, a car salesperson may give an initial price of $20,000 for a vehicle, and the final price you haggle her down to might be $17,000. You may feel good, but in reality, you could have gotten the car for $15,000 had you started at $17,000 and not set the anchor at $20,000. Expectations are the same way, so when I ask if something is attainable, don't shortchange yourself. Ask others who have high expectations of you, look around at other successes, and don't let your fears set your limitations. But always be realistic. On many occasions SEALs have learned this lesson the hard way: we train like supermen only to find out that we are not supermen.

Leverageable

We often set goals thinking that we will accomplish them by ourselves, yet we are significantly more successful if we don't do it alone. We need to find and add *leverage* to help us achieve the results we want. In Chapter 3, I discussed leveraging live ammunition and putting yourself as close to the "X" as you can to add brutal honesty to help accomplish your goals. And in Chapter 10, I talked about the importance of swim buddies. One powerful approach is to commit to achieving your goals to someone else in public. Seek out someone who has done what you want to do and who has your best interests at heart. Find what it is that has a positive effect on your behavior and implement it, such as planning trips to the gym with friends or eating a big meal before shopping for food, so that you are not hungry and buy too much junk food. If I want to get in shape and get healthy, my leverage might be thinking of the "why." For instance, "I want to save my son's daddy" is a compelling way to see my own personal health, and it triggers my love for my son and his well-being.

When I teach foster youth, I tell them that one of the most powerful leveraging tools they have in life is to ask for help. People love to help children, especially the underdogs, and love to pass on their wisdom.

Scary

When we start any new project or set a goal for ourselves, most of us don't address the big elephant in our lives: fear. We usually don't talk about or pay proper attention to what scares us most; we're ashamed of it, among other things. Instead, we focus only on what motivates us, our "why." It's important to understand why you want to do something, but identifying and understanding your fears is also essential. If you don't address the elephant in the room, fear will hang over your head, you will plan with a bad state of mind, and you will carry both the fear and the bad state of mind into the future.

During mission planning, SEALs spend an enormous amount of time addressing all the contingencies and "what-ifs," so when things go wrong, we have an immediate and calculated response. We call these IADs (Immediate Action Drills). If you are patrolling toward a target and get shot at, you don't just make it up as you go. You have an IAD that has been rehearsed over and over. Your reaction is coordinated to maximize your survivability rate, everyone knows what to do, and it works even when the gunfire is loud and you can't hear anything.

> The unknown is often fearsome,
> but planning gives you faith.

SUCCESS UNDER FIRE: CONTINGENCY PLANNING

Our missions can be very complicated, but in general, they all follow a basic format of SMEAC (situation, mission, execution, administration and logistics, and command and control). Let's focus on execution, which has five phases: insert, infiltration, actions at the objective, exfiltration, and extract. During each phase, we try to come up with at least three things that can go wrong, figure out how to mitigate against these, and have an IAD for each of them. I draw three columns, one each for contingencies (what we fear could go wrong), the mitigation, and the IAD (what to do if the fear comes true).

For the first column, imagine you are patrolling along a trail when out of nowhere shots ring out and you find yourself under fire. Now, this can happen during any phase of the mission, and it's one of the worst possible scenarios. You are compromised, and now an enemy of unknown size is firing at you. In the second column, we figure out ways to mitigate this possibility: to patrol to our target, we might choose a path protected by bushes, a place nobody with any sense would go. This is one of our general practices when we move secretly toward an objective; we take the hard route to minimize the possibility of being found by the enemy.

In the third column is the IAD when this event does happen. Shots ring out, and everyone immediately hits the ground in their 360-degree predetermined field of fire. Quickly, the point man fires rapidly in the direction of the enemy, and once he figures out the situation, he yells out the command, "Center peel!" As the point man crawls backward, the next in line starts firing on both sides of the trail, and the entire platoon "zippers" to the rear and takes up a position behind the last man, waiting for the peel to get to them again, much like a wave moving in a stadium. This is done until the platoon gets to a place of cover, which offers a physical barrier. Then someone who finds the cover sets a "door" for everyone to go through, which breaks contact with the enemy and allows the doorman to get a head count. Once safe, the platoon goes silent.

For most of the worst scenarios, we have an IAD that we train and rehearse countless times, so if this happens, we don't have to figure out what to do. There are infinite contingencies that we may encounter on a mission—goat herders, failed equipment, injury, change of mission—but we *must* be prepared. We come up with standard operating procedures so that we all are on the same sheet of music even if we have no communications and things turn really bad, which happens. With such advanced technology today, it's hard to imagine not having communications, but it does happen because technology may fail you in a time of need, so we plan for that, too.

How might you use this contingency planning process in your professional life? Suppose you are giving a presentation to a potential client who would be a big get for your company. When you first receive the assignment, you are incredibly excited that your boss and organization are trusting you to deliver this critical presentation. It may even mean a promotion if you hit a home run! But once your excitement wears off, fear kicks in: fear that you're not a good presenter, that you don't know the information well, that you will lose your train of thought, that technology will fail you, that you will fail and embarrass yourself. Such a significant goal or potential change in our lives (a promotion may be on the line) is almost always scary, which probably means it's what we should be doing.

The key is to create a plan. Think through and rehearse the plan. Make a list of potential contingencies and prepare a mitigation and IAD for each one. Rehearse the IADs, so that when Murphy's law comes to pass, you will know exactly what to do on the spot. The more you can plan for, the higher your confidence, the less you have to worry about, and the greater your chance of success!

Improving Reaction Time: The "Hood Drill"

One of the most powerful drills we have that can be done for many situations is called the "hood drill." We put someone in the center of a large open room with a hood or sack covering his head and upper body. The hood is attached to a ceiling rope or pulley system. An instructor yanks the cord, pulling off the hood, revealing a situation the SEAL must deal with. Sometimes he's armed; sometimes not. It might be dark; it might be loud. There may be several people in the room, with or without weapons. Scenarios are never the same, so the person under the hood learns to react by going on the offensive. This drill teaches you to cut "freeze" times down and respond offensively in a systematic way that will increase your survivability rate, no matter what the scenario. This sort of drill might be extreme for your work or personal life, but it illustrates the concept: preparing your reactions to potential scenarios is an important part of planning that must happen before surprise, speed, and violence of action can carry the day.

You can do such "hood drills" in a business environment by setting up simulations to practice what you would do if a competitor lowered prices or changed course, if a supply chain failed, or if a new product hit the market. Do you think "hood drills" might have helped companies prepare for the consequences of the pandemic? I know it's not quite the same as dealing with someone who might have a loaded weapon, but the idea still works. When you have predetermined responses planned and rehearsed, fear and uncertainty don't rule the situation—you do.

EXERCISE

What is important to you? Set your SEALS goals, prioritize and plan for them, and use the fight triangle to accomplish your missions. Prepare yourself for what may go wrong because it often will.

TAKEAWAYS

- Have a plan. When things go wrong and the pressure is at its greatest, don't rely on innovation; fall back on the plan.

- The fight triangle consists of *surprise, speed,* and *violence of action.*

- Owning the element of surprise—the initiative—can give you superhuman strength against competitors with no control over the situation. Taking the initiative gives you control and puts you on the offensive.

- Use speed to create urgency, motivate others, and develop momentum. It turns others into followers.

- When attacking a project, immerse yourself, commit, obsess—and *do!* Planning, discussing, and preparing are great, but a bias for action and violence of action are necessary for success.

- Organize your to-dos into transformational, transactional, and "f***-that" priorities.

- Our time and attention are finite; be intentional about how you spend them.

- Planning mitigates fear, especially fear of the unknown.

- Goals should be specific, evaluable, actionable and attainable, leverageable, and scary.

- Contingency planning should identify likely contingencies, as well as the mitigation and an IAD (Immediate Action Drill) for each.

12

AWE

Awaken the
Warrior Energy

O ne night I found myself in the back of a helicopter outside the city of Ramadi, Iraq, the most dangerous place on Earth. The aircraft was staged in a remote area of desert, and we were waiting for the call to verify a terrorist for whom we were on the hunt. I had been successful in combat before and was even given a battlefield promotion, a first in Navy SEAL history, to lead this team into the Battle of Al-Anbar. This unit had been training together for a year, but I had just taken over command, so I knew no one. Worse, no one knew me.

The staging area was strategically chosen, close to the target yet far enough away so as not to tip off the terrorist organization. I was seven minutes away from hitting one of the most dangerous targets in my career. This particular high-value target (HVT) had taken all measures to keep his location safe. There was an American tank still burning down the street after trying to make it to this part of town; driving was not an option. The HVT had a heavily armed lookout team, and they moved among schools and mosques to protect them from American attack. The network was paranoid and never stayed very long in one location. The only way to the target was to land on the "X" in the center of the compound, right on the beehive.

With my back against the cockpit looking down the long aisle through my night vision goggles, I could see my SEALs staring at each other, in their own worlds, as we waited for the helicopter to depart. The aircraft was in idle, with its blades turning, and the smell of jet fuel and hydraulic fluid filled the air. This was a moment like I had never had before; I felt like I had a bowling ball in my gut, weighing me down. I was seven minutes away from imminent death or worse, imminent failure, getting someone killed because I screwed up or wasn't ready for this night. It was a true test of GUTS.

Being the Ground Force Commander, I had my headset plugged into the aircraft, listening to the final preparations for departure. From their training, pilots are as calm as monks and speak in a methodical matter-of-fact voice. As they finished their final checks, the helicopter vibrated under power, and the lead pilot checked in with me and said: "Red Bull actual, you have 24 souls on board, seven minutes to target—wheels up." That one word saved my life. He said *souls*, not passengers, not SEALs, not troops, but *souls*. That one word triggered all the training and preparation that I had done in my life and refocused me.

That bowling ball in my gut melted away. The extreme fear that had weighed me down turned into exhilaration, an emotional euphoria that coursed throughout my entire body, mind, and soul. In that moment, I knew that the opposite of fear was love, and at that moment, my focus turned from myself to my team, the men who were trusting their lives to me. One word changed one thought, and that one thought changed everything.

As the pilot increased power, I could feel the helicopter lifting. The last thing I instinctively said over the din came out of me from years of training as a warrior and leader. I yelled down the aisle so everyone could hear, "HOOYAH, mother-f***ers!" That triggered a response from my guys. In unison, they yelled back, "Yeeeeeeeaaaaaa!" For those seven minutes, I was alive like I had never been before. I felt like I was the happiest and most fulfilled person on Earth—all while flying to my potential death.

After that night I tried to understand the meaning of that feeling. I knew that the opposite of fear was love, but that didn't explain it to my satisfaction. Why did I feel the way that I did? What was that feeling? And how do I feel that way again? There was a sense that my ego, my self, had dissolved in those moments. Although I understood the gravity of the situation, that glimpse into the souls of my team produced pure emotional ecstasy. To this day, I am not sure if anyone in that mental state would be considered courageous. Being courageous means acting in the face of fear, but I wasn't fearful that night. I was feeling the opposite, love. It didn't entirely make sense because I didn't know most of the SEALs on that helicopter, but I still loved them.

When I searched for the words to describe what I was feeling, the closest I can come is *agape*. Agape is considered the highest form of love. In the religious context, it refers to God's love for humankind as well as humans' love for God. In its essence, it's goodwill and benevolence toward every living thing. (This may seem ironic given my mission, but I don't decide who lives and who dies—the enemy does. If he puts his hands up, we take him in, but if he puts his hands down on his gun, we take him out.) I believe that all human beings search for agape, even if they don't know what it is, and once they've experienced it, it motivates them toward action for the rest of their lives. It is the purest form of love that *true warriors* know and have felt: the willingness to sacrifice everything to protect others, even if that means losing your life.

In the back of the helicopter that night, I realized that true warriors don't fight for what they hate in front of them; they fight for what they love beside and behind them. I struggled for years after retiring and coming home because I became fueled by hate. Although I knew and had felt agape, I had taken a different path. I became driven by hating my enemy, not allowing myself to let go of that hate, and not allowing myself to awaken my warrior energy. That hate for my enemy was fueled by fear; it was like a disease that took over all aspects of my life. I had lost sight of agape.

The one regret I had in the back of that helicopter that night was that if I were killed, my family and friends would not have known that I didn't die in fear, that I didn't go to my death scared—I went willingly, with a full heart. They would never have known the warmth of fulfillment that washed over me, how I felt privileged to be there, someplace I had never been and would never go again. I knew that not many people were willing and able to be in my seat that night, and that only a few on this Earth were qualified. Out of those qualified, I was *chosen*. I was where I was meant to be, exactly where I wanted to be, doing what I loved, with the people I loved. I was a steward. I was there to lead and to protect.

A LETTER HOME

Before every combat deployment, we SEALs have to get all of our legal matters in order. We fill out powers of attorney, update our wills and, with our next of kin, figure out what IAD our families will take in the event of our deaths. We also write a letter home, a letter that goes with our legal documents that will be opened if we don't return. It's a very emotional process, but the process is a gift because it gives us clarity on the meaning of our lives. Before I go any further, I want to offer you that gift, the chance to write a letter home.

First, on a piece of paper, write down the names of those you want to *see* the letter, and then put that list into an envelope and seal it. Next, put yourself in a comfortable private environment and consider your last words to the world you will leave behind. Allow yourself to explore your thoughts, your memories, your feelings. Then write your letter to your loved ones. If you wish to write several, please do. Put each letter in an envelope and seal it.

What did you say about your life? What did you say to your nearest and dearest? Now, open the first envelope, and see who is not on the list. Why were they not? If you are a leader or work on a team, did you put your people on the list? Did you include the people with whom you spend a large portion of your life? If you want to add to your list, now is a good time to do so.

To me, this is a spiritual reflection exercise: What do I want my life to be? How do I want to spend it? This is the time to let your moral curiosity run freely, explore what it is you stand for, what you want your life's legacy to be. Allow your mind and soul to dream freely without fear, doubt, or ego.

> **Without death, life has no meaning.**

Writing these letters home when you're facing imminent danger is a powerful process of Awakening the Warrior Energy (AWE). It reveals to us how we should be living our lives. Did we give more than we took? Did we have the GUTS to live with agape? Death provides us with a timeline. The problem is that we don't know how much time we have. We have finite space in life's backpack, so what do we fill it with for our life's mission? It's easy to conduct our lives as if the backpack is limitless, and we can just keep filling it without figuring out and prioritizing what is most important until later, but we don't know if we will have a later. We only know that we have a *now*.

> **Living life without a higher purpose is like dancing without music.**

COMING HOME

When I finally came home after years of combat and retired from the SEAL Teams, I realized that being a warrior and going to war creates a lot of moral dissonances. In war, you commit acts that are against your fundamental belief system, and it's natural to feel the lingering pain of guilt, shame, and disgust. I believe that life is the number one value, yet in war, you take it from others and destroy lives forever. Much of the suffering that veterans experience comes from these moral injuries resulting from what they did or didn't do. I have turned the pain of moral injuries and dissonance into something positive.

The first time I took my weapon off safe and was about to pull the trigger during a mission on a dark street in Baghdad, I felt an intense aversion to killing someone, which I felt on the cellular level, beyond the cognizant thought process. Every fiber of my being was driving me not to do it; that feeling proved to me that I was a warrior. True warriors live by the principle to never harm someone unless you have to. Notice that I didn't say "unless they deserve it" because that leads to harmful behavior. *Courageous restraint* is a virtue that every human being should strive for—to empathize with others and to control your actions and emotions. When I look back, I am proud of the fact that I never intentionally harmed someone unless I had to. To those I unintentionally harmed, I am sorry, and I have asked for forgiveness.

The emotional state of mind that writing and reading these letters creates is clarifying. It can help you figure out how you want to live your life and how to lead. You can imagine a lot of people in combat make promises to God or to themselves, "If I get out of this, I promise to (you fill in the blank)." For me, this is a spiritual reflection exercise. What do I want my life to be? What do I fill it with? How do I want to spend it? This is the time to let your moral curiosity run freely, explore what it is you want to stand for, and what you want your life's legacy to be. Allow your mind and soul to dream freely without fear, doubt, or ego.

LEGACY

Great leaders throughout history know that their legacy will live on past death, and it gives them the GUTS to fight for what they believe in on behalf of others. I call this courage the "heroes' high," a feeling of personal responsibility for others, a stewardship of your team and of society as a whole. People like Mother Teresa, Gandhi, and Martin Luther King Jr. were not only great leaders, they were heroes. Once you tap into this way of leading and living, you will tap into agape, and Awaken the Warrior Energy in you. Once you experience this, you will seek it for the rest of your life.

A common mantra in business these days is to "find your why" and do what you are passionate about. Although our why drives us, finding it sounds like a matter of luck, as though we are at the mercy of something other than our own doing. Instead, I say, *create* your why. We are accountable for our own happiness and success. Your passion is not out there. It's inside all of us, waiting to be awakened so it can run free. The purest art in life is how we live our lives, and we alone paint that canvas. It's not given to us at birth. We create it, and the final product is our doing, our GUTS, our legacy.

> Sometimes it takes a long time to
> learn to live as ourselves, but we are
> who we have been waiting for.

ETHOS

In 2005, 70 miles off the coast of Coronado, California, the SEAL Teams held a working group with more than 50 SEALs of different ranks and experiences to once and for all define what a Navy SEAL is and isn't. Our goal was to do a deep assessment of our meaning, purpose, and character as an organization, and capture that in a concise narrative that would serve as a fundamental reference for ourselves, for the rest of the SEAL Teams, and ultimately for those outside the SEAL forces to better understand who we are, how we think, what we do, and what we stand for. It would become our ethos.

Two wars had taken a toll on the organization, and the stress of that burden exposed the seams of our cultural character. War is the ultimate arena in life and will test who you are as a human being and as an organization. All academic courses in ethics and leadership will fail you in times of stress in combat if you genuinely don't have them defined, understood, accepted, rehearsed, internalized, and worked intimately into your culture and your soul. When you build an ethos, you have a specific blueprint for who you are, how you think, what you do, and what you stand for instinctively guiding you through life.

Our expression "you fight like you train" means that whatever you train to becomes you, and when the fear and stress get dialed up, you will fall back on your training. Character, leadership, and teamwork are no different. In times of stress at or near the "X" in life, you will find out who you really are and what you actually believe. You don't act one way at home and another at work; your character doesn't know the difference.

Our SEALs came off the island after a week of grappling with what *is* and what *is not* a Navy SEAL, and they brought back our first stated ethos:

> In times of war or uncertainty there is a special breed of warrior ready to answer our Nation's call. A common man with uncommon desire to succeed. Forged by adversity, he stands alongside America's finest special operations forces to serve his country, the American people, and protect their way of life. I am that man.
>
> My Trident is a symbol of honor and heritage. Bestowed upon me by the heroes that have gone before, it embodies the trust of those I have sworn to protect. By wearing the Trident I accept the responsibility of my chosen profession and way of life. It is a privilege that I must earn every day.
>
> My loyalty to Country and Team is beyond reproach. I humbly serve as a guardian to my fellow

Americans always ready to defend those who are unable to defend themselves. I do not advertise the nature of my work, nor seek recognition for my actions. I voluntarily accept the inherent hazards of my profession, placing the welfare and security of others before my own.

I serve with honor on and off the battlefield. The ability to control my emotions and my actions, regardless of circumstance, sets me apart from other men. Uncompromising integrity is my standard. My character and honor are steadfast. My word is my bond.

We expect to lead and be led. In the absence of orders I will take charge, lead my teammates, and accomplish the mission. I lead by example in all situations.

I will never quit. I persevere and thrive on adversity. My Nation expects me to be physically harder and mentally stronger than my enemies. If knocked down, I will get back up, every time. I will draw on every remaining ounce of strength to protect my teammates and to accomplish our mission. I am never out of the fight.

We demand discipline. We expect innovation. The lives of my teammates and the success of our mission depend on me—my technical skill, tactical proficiency, and attention to detail. My training is never complete.

We train for war and fight to win. I stand ready to bring the full spectrum of combat power to bear in order to achieve my mission and the goals established by my country. The execution of my duties will be swift and violent when required yet guided by the very principles that I serve to defend.

Brave men have fought and died building the proud tradition and feared reputation that I am bound to uphold. In the worst of conditions, the legacy of my teammates steadies my resolve and silently guides my every deed. I will not fail.

During this battle to create the ethos—and yes, it *was* a battle—we had more than a few disagreements. The main point of contention centered on the SEAL code, the distillation of the ethos that all SEALs carry in their wallets to review as needed contains the statement: "train for war, fight to win, defeat our Nation's enemies." In the ethos, it states, "achieve my mission and the goals established by my country." An important difference of opinion emerged over a single word: *defeat.*

We had two schools of thought: one that preferred the phrase "we *defeat* our Nation's enemies" and the other that favored "we *destroy* our Nation's enemies." The choice of a single word made a world of difference: it would paint a distinctly different self-image, as well as a different understanding of what we do as our nation's top warriors. It may seem insignificant to you, but when the stress dial gets turned up as we approach the "X," this word matters, and it matters a lot. To me, the image evoked by the word *destroy* is extremely violent and hateful. Being a "destroyer" makes me judge, jury, and executioner. Such a self-image can lead you into a dark cave of moral hazards that becomes hard to navigate out of. Words matter!

As a warrior and leader, I am not harmless, but I choose to be a gentle man, a *gentleman*. In all aspects of my life, I will act with courageous restraint fueled by agape, not the hatred that I once was filled with. When I contemplate this battle around the words *destroy* and *defeat* and how *defeat* was finally chosen, it reinforces what I felt in that helicopter. It tells me how to live my life, how to lead, and how to be a better human being. It demands that I have the GUTS to have restraint, to be a steward, and to lead myself and others with agape.

MAKING YOUR PERSONAL ETHOS

You may already have an ethos by which you live. It may be a spiritual ethos. It may be a work ethos. It may be an organizational ethos, like that of the SEAL Teams. If you have such a group ethos in place, then you're a step ahead. It will help you craft your personal ethos. If you're not part of a larger team that has an ethos, you can develop one of your own. It can be very simple; something like the Golden Rule or a short list of "I will always" and "I will never" statements. Or it can be a more elaborate framework of personal values and guiding principles that guide your being and behavior.

My ethos is the energy that fuels my actions, life, and leadership. When you awaken this warrior energy, you will find the GUTS you seek, the transformation you've dreamed of. This AWE will motivate you to greatness in times of darkness and despair.

For Whom the Bell Tolls

On the Naval Amphibious Base in Coronado, California, in a small, enclosed area for BUD/S training that we call the "grinder," is an unassuming brass bell hanging from a post, with a braided rope hanging from the tongue of the bell. The grinder is sacred ground to all SEALs because we all shed blood, sweat, and tears on that very ground.

All students coming through BUD/S training know this simple rule: at any time they can, without penalty, walk up to the bell, take hold of the braided rope, ring it three times, and leave BUD/S training forever. Throughout the training, you can hear the bell ring out loud, audible up and down the beach, and heads turn slightly toward the bell as the student departs. They know that student will be leaving his helmet in a long row of helmets of former students who also decided that being a SEAL was not for them. The bell is a definitive statement of the student's commitment to leaving the program and the SEAL way of life. For a short period, the bell was removed because some critics believed that it was a mark of disgrace to have to ring a bell, announcing to everyone in earshot that you were leaving the program. But SEALs demanded that it be returned, and it was. The bell had taken on significance to the community and had become an integral part of SEAL culture. The critics didn't understand that the bell is *not* a quitter's bell; the bell is a commitment bell for those who commit to leaving the program. There is no disgrace in leaving, and when a student chooses to go and ring the bell, we encourage him to ring it like he means it, to ring it loud!

As a consequence, this bell is a symbol that has an essential place in our culture. And, indeed, you cannot un-ring a bell. Much of our modern world is ambiguous, and most people are ambivalent about many of the important issues in their lives. They go through their days half-asleep, uncaring, committed more to a paycheck than to any purpose or goal of the organization they are part of, or even to their own goals and their own purpose. Ring the bell and commit to a life worth living, one that *you* design, one that is truly honest and authentic with yourself and with the world. By doing so, you create your why for living, fueled by GUTS and agape. You will never hate what you do when you are who you were meant to be!

The principles in this book are meant to transform you, but you must ring the bell, you must commit, and that commitment starts with your ethos. So who are you? What do you stand for?

I challenge you to look down the aisle of your own helicopter in life, stare at the souls around you, and explore what your life can be and how you can lead yourself and others with agape. Develop your own ethos, write it down, ring the bell, commit to it, and then practice it in every aspect of your life. So that when the bell does toll for thee, you know that your letter home matches your life and your ethos, and those reading it can honor and respect you for living the life that you chose and designed, a life that takes GUTS!

NOTES

Introduction
1. Elbert Hubbard, "A Message to Garcia," 1899, available at MIT Computer, Science and Artificial Intelligence Laboratory, https://courses.csail.mit.edu/6.803/pdf/hubbard1899.pdf.

Chapter 1
1. "Adult Obesity Facts," Centers for Disease Prevention and Control, 2020, https://www.cdc.gov/obesity/data/adult.html.
2. "All the World's Wealth in One Visual," howmuch.net, 2020, https://howmuch.net/articles/distribution-worlds-wealth-2019.

Chapter 3
1. "Everyone Thinks They Are Above Average," CBS News, 2013, https://www.cbsnews.com/news/everyone-thinks-they-are-above-average/.
2. Oxford Reference.com, https://www.oxfordreference.com/view/10.1093/acref/9780191826719.001.0001/q-oro-ed4-00003457.

Chapter 5
1. Friedrich Nietzsche, *The Twilight of the Idols*, translated by A.M. Ludovici. London, England: T.N. Foulis, 1911. https://www.gutenberg.org/files/52263/52263-h/52263-h.htm.

Chapter 7

1. "Sitting Will Kill You, Even if You Exercise," CNN.com, 2015, https://www.cnn.com/2015/01/21/health/sitting-will-kill-you/index.html.
2. "How Humans Are Polluting the World with Noise," Made for Minds, dw.com, https://www.dw.com/en/how-humans-are-polluting-the-world-with-noise/a-42945885#:~:text=%22The%20day%20will%20come%20when,streets%20of%20Germany's%20capital%20Berlin.
3. Lt. General Mark Hertling, Army, TEDxMidAtlantic, 2012, https://www.youtube.com/watch?v=sWN13pKVp9s.
4. Rafeal de Cabo and Mark Mattson, "Effects of Intermittent Fasting on Health, Aging, and Disease," *The New England Journal of Medicine*, Dec. 26, 2019, https://www.nejm.org/doi/full/10.1056/nejmra1905136.
5. "How Much Sugar Do You Eat?," New Hampshire Department of Health and Human Services, https://www.dhhs.nh.gov/dphs/nhp/documents/sugar.pdf.
6. Siri Carpenter, "That Gut Feeling," American Psychological Association, 2012, https://www.apa.org/monitor/2012/09/gut-feeling#:~:text=Gut%20bacteria%20also%20produce%20hundreds,both%20mood%20and%20GI%20activity.
7. "1 in 3 Adults Don't Get Enough Sleep," Centers for Disease Control and Prevention, 2016, https://www.cdc.gov/media/releases/2016/p0215-enough-sleep.html.

Chapter 8

1. Marcel Schwantes, "Study: 60 Percent of Employees Are More Likely to Suffer a Heart Attack if Their Bosses Have These Traits," *Inc.*, 2017, https://www.inc.com/marcel-schwantes/study-60-percent-of-employees-are-more-likely-to-s.html#:~:text=and%20Environmental%20Medicine.-,Researchers%20studied%20more%20than%203%2C100%20men%20over%20a%2010%2Dyear,They%20were%20inconsiderate.
2. Rebecca Keegan, "Bradley Cooper on 'American Sniper,'" *Los Angeles Times*, 2015, https://www.latimes.com/entertainment/envelope/la-en-0212-bradley-cooper-20150212-story.html.

Chapter 9

1. Kim Gittleson, "World's Fair: Isaac Asimov's Predictions 50 Years On," BBC News, 2014, https://www.bbc.com/news/technology-27069716.

INDEX

Fear, 12–14, 18–19, 29–30, 151
 brain response to, 15–17, 20
 defeatist language causing, 88
 focus on, 82–83
 love compared to, 239–240
 noise causing, 127
 physical responses, 20–21
 in planning, 229–230
 public speaking and, 14, 28
 of writing, 27–29
Fear-based state of mind, 147, 152–153,
 193
Feedback, 96, 110–111, 122
Field, Sally, 154
Fight triangle, 218–222, 234
Fight-or-flight, 103–104, 127, 179
First, Fast, Fearless (Hiner), vii, ix–x, 24,
 142–143
First strike language, 89–90, 167
First strike mindset, 78–79, 88, 93
Fitbit, 110
Focus, 97, 113
 distractions effecting, 66–67, 75, 175
 on fear, 82–83
 immersion improving, 66–67
 listening, 74, 212–214
 meditation improving, 67–68
 on others, 202–203
 present, 63–64, 69, 73
 race car driving and, 61–62
 shifting, 70–71
Focus discipline, 64, 83
Focus thieves, 64–65
Force, in fight triangle, 221–222
Forrest Gump (film), 122
Fox walk, 72–73
Frankl, Viktor, 150–151, 157
Frogmen. *See* Naked Warriors
Front sight focus, 62–63
Full concentration on a single act
 (Ichigyo Zammai), 69
Future focus, 63–64
Future mind training, 171, 175–178

G
Galatea effect, 89
Garcia, Calixto, 6–7

Geneva Convention, 200
Genius, 170–171
Geographical orientation, 77–78
Gilbert, Dan, 37
Goals, 40–41, 64, 170, 235
 leverageable, 228–229
 SEALS model for, 225–230
 transformational, 65–66, 191
 weaknesses turned into, 56–57
Good habits, 43, 99, 100–101, 113, 196
Graduates, SEALs, 3–4, 126, 141
Gratitude, 83–85, 102, 186, 196–198
Grit (Duckworth), 171
Ground Force Commander, 238
Guam, 190
Guinness World Records, 179
Gut, as second brain, 131–132
Guugu Yimithirr (aboriginal tribe),
 77–78

H
Habits, 96, 129, 156, 222–223
 bad, 59, 99
 effects of, 123, 124, 129
 good, 43, 99, 100–101, 113, 196
 "Habitudes," 23, 30, 100
Halo effect, 170–171
Hamlet (Shakespeare), 153
Hanks, Tom, 122
Happiness, 24–25, 150, 157
 "Hard" (physical and mental condition),
 127, 138
Hate, 240, 248
Hawthorne Effect, 202
Health, 117–118, 132, 135–136
 state of mind and, 153–154, 157
Heart attacks, 148
Hell Week, 2, 91–92, 102
 delayed gratification during, 99–100
 sleep deprivation, 63–64, 132–133
Hemingway, Ernest, viii
Hertling, Mark, 128
High-value target (HVT), 237–238
Hillel the Elder, 43
Hippocampus, 17
History Channel, 58
Hitting the surf, 91–92, 96

ABOUT THE AUTHOR

Ed Hiner is a genuine hero of the global war on terrorism. In his 20-year career as a Navy SEAL, he made nine major deployments on five continents, half of which were combat tours. Twice awarded the Bronze Star with V for valor and combat leadership, Hiner commanded hundreds of direct combat missions and low-visibility operations in Iraq, Afghanistan, Southeast Asia, and Central America.

Born and raised in Virginia's Blue Ridge Mountains, Hiner grew up with a thirst for competition, and he developed an indomitable will to win that would serve him well in his life's work as a warrior and leader. His talent earned him a scholarship to Virginia Commonwealth University, where he was a Division One baseball player. During a holiday break from college in Virginia Beach, Hiner spent a day helping out a Navy wife who was being forced from her home while her husband was deployed to the Persian Gulf. On a trip to her storage unit, Hiner met an active duty Navy SEAL who volunteered to help. The ensuing day-long conversation provided Hiner (who had never heard of the SEALs) with the spark he needed. He hitchhiked back to Richmond, went straight to the U.S. Navy recruiter, and enlisted.

Hiner graduated from the Basic Underwater Demolition/ SEAL (BUD/S) training in 1993 with class 189. Prior to the terrorist attacks of September 11, 2001, Hiner deployed several times as an enlisted SEAL Operator. He was then picked to attend Officer Candidate School where he earned his commission as a distinguished honor graduate and class president. Following that, Hiner earned a master's degree in executive leadership from the University of San Diego. He went on to make numerous deployments as a SEAL Officer.

Shortly after 9/11, Hiner was selected to integrate directly into the elite British Special Boat Service (SBS), where he served as Executive Officer and Task Force Black team member at the height of the Iraq War and follow-on counterinsurgency efforts. For his efforts while serving in Task Force Black, Hiner was specially promoted to Lieutenant Commander and given command of his own SEAL Task Unit, which deployed to Ramadi at the peak of the Iraq insurgency. This was the first time in the history of the SEAL Teams that a Lieutenant was promoted to Lieutenant Commander for the express purpose of leading a specific combat deployment.

Throughout his SEAL career, Hiner felt it imperative that he continually pass along what he had learned. In addition to his combat tours, in his role as a Navy Special Warfare Training Officer, Hiner was responsible for shaping, training, and qualifying hundreds of Navy SEALs. He has trained students at the BUD/S school; he has trained the trainers who train the students; he has been the officer in charge of training at the BUD/S school; and he has managed all basic and advanced training for West Coast SEAL Teams, and then for all Navy SEALs. He has trained all SEAL Team members to be leaders. He is among the most experienced SEAL trainers in the history of the organization.

Hiner is the *Los Angeles Times* bestselling author of *First, Fast, Fearless: How to Lead Like a Navy SEAL* and a contributor to the *San Diego Union Tribune*. He is featured in the books *Leading at a Higher Level* by Ken Blanchard and *The Sheriff of Ramadi* by Dick Couch, as well as in The History Channel documentary series *Navy SEALs: America's Secret Warriors.*

Through The Hiner Group, he draws on this vast experience as a coach and consultant specializing in leadership, team building, mental toughness, resilience, and self-leadership. A highly sought-after keynote speaker for corporate events, he is the ethos officer and mental toughness coach for the professional basketball team, the San Diego Guardians. Hiner is also the founder and president of Asymmetrical Evolution, a youth education company dedicated to underserved youth in San Diego, California, and throughout the country.

He lives with his wife, Wendy, and son, Jake, in La Jolla, California.

For more information, visit edhiner.com.